D1143002

His Name is Rebecca

REBECCA DE HAVALLAND

WITH EVELYN WALSH

POOLBEG

Published 2010
by Poolbeg Books Ltd.
123 Grange Hill, Baldoyle,
Dublin 13, Ireland
Email: poolbeg@poolbeg.com

© Rebecca De Havalland
Evelyn Walsh 2010

The moral right of the author has been asserted.

Copyright for typesetting, layout, design
© Poolbeg Books Ltd.

A catalogue record for this book is available from the British Library.

ISBN 978-1-84223-444-0

All rights reserved. No part of this publication may be reproduced or transmitted in any form or by any means, electronic or mechanical, including photography, recording, or any information storage or retrieval system, without permission in writing from the publisher. The book is sold subject to the condition that it shall not, by way of trade or otherwise, be lent, resold or otherwise circulated without the publisher's prior consent in any form of binding or cover other than that in which it is published and without a similar condition, including this condition, being imposed on the subsequent purchaser.

Hair by Patrick Kazz@globalhairacadamy.com

Typeset by Patricia Hope in Sabon

Printed by
CPI Cox & Wyman, UK

www.poolbeg.com

Note on the authors

Rebecca De Havalland was born in Granard, Co Longford, Ireland, in 1958. Rebecca became one of the top hair and make-up artists in Ireland and the UK. She was the first Irish person to have gender reassignment surgery in 1989. Rebecca now lives in Dublin where she has established a model agency. De Havalland Model Management. This is her first book.

Evelyn Walsh has been writing since 2004. She was nominated for a Hennessey First Fiction award in 2007. This is her first published book.

Acknowledgements

I would like to thank Pat Prizeman and Yvonne Kinsella, Literary Agents, for prodding me to write this book and then selling the concept of it to the lovely people in Poolbeg Press. Thanks also to writer Evelyn Walsh, and editors Gaye Shortland and Brian Langan, for their assistance in the writing of this book.

There are so many other people I have to acknowledge, both in Ireland and the UK, that I quite simply cannot list them. I'd be sure to unintentionally leave someone out, feelings might be hurt and that would never do. But special mention must be made of Shane McCarthy, photographer, for his belief in me and my work, and of course all the crew at Team De Havalland for all their hard work and for bringing a breath of fresh air into my life.

I especially want to thank my family and all my friends. Each and every one of you know who you are and I thank you all.

*For my daughter and
granddaughter*

CONTENTS

"There are more things in heaven
and earth, Horatio,
Than are dreamt of in your philosophy"

Hamlet Act 1 Sc v
WILLIAM SHAKESPEARE

There was a little girl
Who had a little curl
Right in the middle of her forehead
And when she was good, she was very
very good
And when she was bad she was horrid.

Nursery Rhyme
H W LONGFELLOW

Preface

Before I agreed to write this book I thought long and hard about why I wanted to tell my story to the world, open my heart and soul, make my life an open book. My literary agents and friends drove me mad, asking: "Are you ready for this? All the publicity and talk? Your whole life being laid out in front of everyone?" What stupid questions! How can I be ready for something that I live every day? Be ready for something that *is*. This *is* my life. This book tells my life story to date. What I have done in my life – my thoughts, feelings and words about those things I have done and about other things that have been done to me. For over forty-five years I have been on a rollercoaster; I now feel that the rollercoaster is slowing down – finally running smoothly into those last few level metres of track – and that the path my life has taken over the last two years will continue, that the good fortune and love that has finally come into my life will remain.

People can be patronising, without realising it I'm sure, when talking to those who are different. I know people are trying to be kind when they try to identify with me, saying: "Oh, I have a friend or a family member who is gay or bisexual or transvestite or a drag-queen." Hello! I'm not that friend, no more than you are. I'm me.

There are those among us who presume to know others and 'understand' them. None of us should do that; empathise yes, fine, great – it is the loving and Christian thing to do. But you ain't been me, honey, you ain't gone through the things that I've gone through, you ain't walked in my shoes. No more than I have walked in yours. It is a miracle that I am still here; still battling, still living.

My story is a story of survival, against all sorts of odds and prejudices. Please, I do not want to be 'understood'. I do not want sympathy. Poor Rebecca, sad Rebecca. I am not a freak, some strange creature needing to be examined, studied, talked about. I simply want to *be*. Like you, I want to live my life, work and be with my family, just like everyone of us – to get on with my life.

Hence the book. Next time somebody asks me questions about my life, very personal questions, I'll tell them buy this book. It's all in this book. R.T.F.M. – Read The F****** Manual!

I don't know whether I come from a family – or perhaps it is a national trait – where everything is brushed under the carpet. In the past we Irish brushed so much under the carpet that we ended up with this big pile of dust and dirt – hidden things, forgotten things, let's-not-talk-about-it things – shit – just lying there in the middle of the floor waiting to trip us all up. We closed our eyes, ears, minds. Hear no evil, see no evil, speak no evil. If only we could all just tell the truth and accept each other's truths. We cannot hurt each other with the truth.

To me my life is simply that: my life. Nothing extraordinary. It is what I wake up to each morning and sometimes it is what I cry myself to sleep over at night. I take up more or less the same body-space as you. I am a similar jumble of atoms, molecules, cells, bones, flesh, thoughts, words, memories and feelings as you. So you see, I am not so very different to you. A slight tweak here, a lift there, a different set of experiences and you could be moulded into me, or I into you.

I am not naïve. I do realise that the path my life has taken has been more confusing at times than the paths of others. Now is the right time for me to write this book. I could not have written it before this. My life has come full circle, and if this book can colour in that circle and explain to the world what life has been like for me then I will have succeeded. Perhaps this book will help others, guide them without fear or despair into acceptance of themselves. Some of the memories I had to relive to write this book have been extraordinarily painful, but in ways I am glad of that pain, for now I can put the memories behind me and move on with the rest of my life.

In an effort to protect family and friends, who may not feel as comfortable as I do with who I am or what I have done, I have changed some names. If I have hurt anyone by either inclusion or exclusion from this memoir then I apologise. There was never any hurt intended to anyone. All our lives are too short and far too precious for such hurtfulness. I have been blunt and honest about the last fifty-two years. I hope to live the rest of the years allotted to me in this same honest light.

Let's get one thing straight.

I'm not gay.
I'm not a transvestite.
I'm not a transsexual.
I'm commonly called transgender.
If you insist on a label – I'm medically classified with Gender Identity Dysphoria.
A third gender.
But –
I am a woman.
I love my family, my daughter, my granddaughter.
I love my many friends, my little dog, my home.
I love my work and I'm bloody good at what I do.
I am Irish and consider myself a good citizen.
I am a Christian.
I live and breathe and love and laugh – just like you.
I wash and dress and walk and eat and sleep – just like you.
I am just like you.
I have been to Hell and back. Survived.
I am me.
But in the beginning . . . . . .

1

Welcome to the World Baby Boy

I was born Eamon Tallon on June 6th 1958, the second child and first son of a middle-class family in Granard, County Longford. My mother's family were relatively well-to-do, owning land and several properties and running the local shop where everyone bought their groceries. This was a poorer – much poorer – Ireland than today and these possessions did make us that little bit different, I suppose. My sister Lucy was fourteen months old when I was born and my brother Michael came along a year after me. As small children we were close and played together happily. I'm sure we squabbled, but to be honest I don't think there were many tiffs.

Those early years in Granard are very important to me. I often return to them in my thoughts and smile, for they were, without doubt, the happiest and most stable time of my life. Whenever I'm in trouble, particularly when I am soul-troubled, it is to Granard I run, either in person or in my thoughts. I am always, always accepted back – sometimes with a sigh and a wry smile but the town takes me back and I feel loved there.

On three separate occasions I have set up businesses there. They all failed in the end because I would get restless and need to move on. But my heart and soul belong in Granard. A sleepy little midlands town where everyone knows everyone else. It keeps an eye on the comings and goings of all its sons and daughters, and keeps a place in its heart for us all.

When I look at some friends, people whose lives have been every bit as confusing and fractured as mine, I can see a stability in me that is absent in their lives. I owe this purely to those first years in Granard. Don't they say that the first four years of your life are the most important? I truly do not think I would still be alive if it were not for the grounding my immediate and extended family gave me in those early years.

My maternal grandfather died a relatively young man and my mother was only six when he passed away. This left the responsibility of both rearing a family and trying to sublet land and properties the family owned to my grandmother. My mother was a lot younger than her siblings and the older ones would have been old enough to help out in the shop and in running the business. But I don't think Granny would have been particularly prepared for any of this – women at that time didn't 'do' business, not middle class women anyway. It must have been tough on her. But Granny's character was incredibly strong. She was a tough old bird, she had to be.

A woman's place in the society of a 1930s and 40s rural Irish town was very definitely in the home. Not running businesses, not going to marts or managing money. But Granny did all of it . . . maybe not the marts? No, I can't see Granny having done marts – she had a very particular notion of her position in the societal hierarchy of the town and its hinterlands, and I doubt attending marts would have enhanced that position – at least not in her eyes!

By the time I was born Mum's sister Maureen and her husband Pat, who were civil servants, were running the local Labour Exchange in the town. Another of her sisters, Sybil, lived in Dublin with her family. I mention these two women particularly because they were very, very important people in my life and I loved them dearly.

Life in rural Ireland is, even today, blessedly sleepy and quiet, although we didn't think of it like that when we were children. St Mary's Catholic Church in Granard dominates the town, for it sits at the top of the hill and can be seen from almost any place there. It is a beautiful Gothic church, built around 1862, with an architecturally theatrical and commanding exterior. Inside, it is a very peaceful space, well lit through beautiful stained-glass windows and with a stunning and elaborate timber roof structure. It is regarded as one of the finest of its type in this country – well worth a visit for anyone interested in either churches or architecture. I love that church. From the time I was very small I always felt safe in it. During Lent, as soon as I was old enough, I used to run up the hill on my own and go to Mass every morning before school. When I came home, Granny would boil me an egg for my breakfast and tell me I was a "little topper". I loved that attention and strove to be good all the time. The steep road down from the church was the perfect place on winter's icy mornings for all the children of the town to slide down on plastic coats or turf bags. A terrace of houses comes down the hill from the church and it was at the bottom of this hill that my grandmother's house and shop stood. The 'Corner House' we called it, and from the upstairs gable room of that house we could look out the window and see all the comings and goings on Main Street.

That was always my favourite room in the house. I would drape the net curtains over my head and pretend I was a good friend of the Virgin Mary. I also recollect praying, as a very young child, that when I woke up the next morning I would have changed into a girl overnight.

I am often asked when did I realise I was a girl. I always knew I was a girl. It had nothing to do with 'thought' there was no process of realisation. What I now know is that all my instincts were feminine: the way girls perceive themselves, feel about others, interact with other kids. But I could never have worded it like that in 1960s, 70s or even 80s Ireland.

Our Lady's statue in the gable room of that house

stood on a shelf above a little platform, the platform concealing a cistern, I think. As children we used this platform as a stage and I loved performing on it: singing, dancing or in little made up plays with Lucy, Michael and friends. It is to the safeness and security of that room that I would go if ever anything bothered me. I have a great devotion to Our Blessed Lady all my life I have felt that no matter what I did she still loved me, and through her so did her son, Jesus Christ. My faith is my constancy and has been my friend through all the dark days.

We played out on the street and up on the little hills behind the church, near a grotto devoted to St Bernadette and Our Lady of Lourdes.

Twenty years after we played there, in January 1984, a fifteen-year-old girl called Anne Lovett died giving birth alone to a 'secret' baby. Poor darling children. It was a ferocious scandal at the time and a media scrum descended on Granard. Sleepy little Granard had never seen such publicity. People outside of the town found it hard to believe that such a thing could happen in a 'modern' society – and the town itself felt under siege, as if each and every individual in it was to blame.

There were tunnels (or that's what we called them) above the grotto where we'd say a prayer to Our Lady and then scamper around playing hide-and-seek, 'Batman and Robin', 'Cowboys and Indians', chasing games and skipping games. We did all the normal things small children did back then: tennis, a favourite in the summer, and fishing, in the nearby Lough Gowna. I was a very effeminate child and loved games that reflected the family, like 'Mammies and Daddies', house or tea parties. I loved 'Doctors and Nurses' as well. I liked things to be neat and tidy and wasn't an obstreperous youngster. I did play with boys but not particularly 'boy' games. I had no interest in football, for example, although we all would have kicked a ball about, girls and boys together. Just playing, being kids.

Within the pub, the home and school, the three main topics of conversation for young and old alike were the Church, the GAA and the neighbours. Granard's most famous son at that time was Larry Cunningham, a local man who had his own showband, The Mighty Avons. They were kings of the showband circuit in Ireland and the UK and everyone in Granard loved the fact that the town had produced such a star. In later years Eddie Macken, the Irish show jumper, was another Granard boy who made good and the Horse Show in Dublin's RDS was a 'must-go' for the society ladies of Granard!

Kitty Kiernan, the love of the brave and handsome Irish Freedom Fighter Michael Collins, was a Granard girl; if you visit The Greville Arms – the town's hotel – you can still see many pictures and memorabilia mounted on the walls in tribute to these star-crossed lovers. We were brought up on tales of them and of the uprising in Ireland in 1916, when men like Michael Collins and Eamon De Valera fought for Irish freedom. In fact, I was named after Eamon De Valera. We were proud to be Irish and proud to have a connection to one of the leaders of that uprising – the fact that both

Michael Collins and Kitty Kiernan were young and good-looking made them even more appealing to us children. We thought their love story and Michael Collins's death by ambush at Béal na mBláth in County Cork in 1922 were terribly romantic. My Uncle Tom in particular would talk to us about the English and how the Irish Republican Army had fought them and taken Ireland back for us, the Irish people. He talked of the Black & Tans and how people feared and hated them. Uncle Tom was a great storyteller and we could listen to him for hours.

In writing about this time of my life I realise that a lot of my story will be a jumble of half-remembered images, smells and sounds; but I never intended to write a linear personal history anyway – there has been nothing linear about my life! This memoir is rather a personal idiosyncratic look at my life.

In childhood we are too young to analyse and understand all that goes on, but I do know that I felt happy; loving Mum, Granny and my family. My memories of those early years are of happiness and stability. But, in fact, my parents' marriage was in trouble by the time I was born – all the usual problems, I suppose, and two strong personalities pulling against each other instead of with each other. My father, Brendan, who was a mechanic, left the family home in the early 60s. I only saw him a couple of times after that when I was in my early teens. I did attempt to make his funeral in London decades later – to be sure that he was dead – but more of that later.

From then on, Mum's family were very influential in our upbringing. We moved in with my grandmother and she became our primary carer. We loved them – Granny and all our aunts and uncles and cousins. Mum was Granny's baby and we were her baby's babies so Granny looked after us all. Granny was strict but we loved her to bits – she was our constancy. Mum was a good-looking woman and lively by all accounts. As the youngest of her own family she had been everybody's darling growing up. Mum must have found it very hard being left with three small children to rear alone. But we never wanted for anything. Not materially anyway. Always clean and neat with warm clothes, good shoes and coats, good home-cooked dinners and access to books and education.

Life for a deserted wife is always difficult; but in small-town Ireland (we are but a village) in the early 1960s it was incredibly hard. The Church frowned on broken marriages and the State couldn't or wouldn't help those caught in these situations. It always fell back on extended family to keep the innocent victims of marriage fall-out as safe as they could. All this meant that my brother, sister and I were very closely bound. I only have very vague memories of my dad; I sometimes wonder if the smell of tobacco on a checked sports jacket and the jingle of coins in a pocket that I do remember are memories of him at all.

The fact that my father left and no longer supported

us financially meant that my mother had to work to care for us. So Mum was away a lot. She worked away from home with a catering firm that looked after the meal needs of the members of the religious orders and other groups like the Jesuits and the Freemasons in Dublin. For our early years Mum seemed to be this exotic, beautiful stranger who dipped in and out of our lives on special occasions like Christmas, birthdays and the odd weekend. I would always feel excited when I'd hear she was coming, for she always brought sweets or presents – I suppose to make up for not being there during the week. My admiration for my mum was at a very superficial level. I loved her for what she brought me. She wasn't there for me to love her for anything else. Not through any fault of hers, I know – she had to work.

So, as I said, Granny became our primary carer through those early years, ably assisted by our relatives about the town. Aunt Maureen and Uncle Pat in particular were very central in our lives; they had no children of their own and rather doted on us. We hopped and trotted between the Corner House and Aunty Maureen's house further down the Main Street. So my love, the daily love, went to Granny, my sister and brother, little friends about the town and our aunts and uncles. Granny was the most prominent person in my early life. I adored her and she doted on me because I was a polite and neat little boy who was always willing to please. I bent over backwards to make her love me, make anyone love me.

Good moments with my mother were rare and all the more cherished because of that. The most vivid image I have of Mum in those early years is of one afternoon during a holiday in Courtown, a seaside town in County Wexford. Granny was from Wexford originally and we would visit her relatives there in summer. I remember one particular summer's day. It was a lovely day, warm and sunny, and I was lying on grass looking at a ladybird crawling along a blade of grass, the blade barely moving under her weight. I loved her colours and the red shiny shell of her tiny, tiny body with its black spots fascinated me. I looked across the field and saw my mum walking back from the local farmhouse, carrying a pail of milk. She moved like a dancer; her long blonde hair lifting in the breeze. She was wearing a lemon dress with a fitted bodice and a full skirt that day – a much-favoured dress. It had a pattern of pink roses on it and I had never, ever, seen anyone as beautiful. You know the way sometimes you look at someone and you just feel a big surge of love for them in that particular moment? I think that was the first time I felt that, looking at this beautiful woman and being so completely proud that she was my mum.

Another vivid childhood memory is of one Christmas – asking Santa to bring me "the biggest teddy bear in the world" – I may have been four or five years of age. On Christmas Eve that year there was a bit of a kerfuffle, some confusion – it had been snowing, I think, or raining heavily, and Mum was on the bus coming back from Dublin. I can't remember if the bus broke down or got stuck in snow, but I know Granny was worrying because Mum was so late and she chased us off to bed. I only realised in later years that no doubt the Santa presents were on the bus too. I remember poor Lucy was incredibly sick at the time, too weak to even climb the stairs, and Uncle Pat had to carry her up to her bedroom. We were bitterly disappointed at not being allowed to stay up to greet Mum and see what she brought us.

When I got up and ran downstairs on Christmas morning there was an enormous, slightly damp, teddy bear in the chair beside the range. I'm smiling as I write because I remember distinctly that little flutter of joy in my stomach when I saw it. I turned to look at Mum and she was standing with her back to the kitchen door, her head framed by the white red-edged fabric of the roller towel that hung there. She was laughing and crying at the same time at my reaction. I couldn't believe Santa had brought this huge teddy bear all the way from the North Pole for me. I thought I must have been the best boy all year to deserve such a present.

In November 1963, I was in the kitchen playing tea parties in front of the range with my sister's dolls and my teddies when Mum and Granny both screamed. Mum dropped the dinner plate she had been drying and I got a terrible fright – I thought Granny would go mad because her good china plate was in a million pieces.

"Oh, Lord save us and bless us! That poor man – and his lovely wife and children!" Granny was shaking her hands and moaning "Oh! Oh! Oh!", her hands all sudsy from the dishwater and little drops of water and suds going everywhere. The news had just come over the radio that John F Kennedy had been assassinated in Dallas, Texas. Mum and Granny were crying and even I, at five, understood the momentous nature of this man's death. One of our own, our tribe, our family, was dead. Pictures of JFK, the Pope and the Sacred Heart (with the votive candle always flickering in front of it) adorned practically every Irish home of that time, plus little statuettes of course: the Child of Prague was a great favourite (essential for putting out in the garden the night before your wedding – to ward off rain!), the Virgin Mary (my favourite), St Bernadette of Lourdes (my second favourite) and St Therese of Lisieux, the Little Flower. These saintly creatures and JFK were our heroes and now JFK had gone to meet them all in Heaven. I was devastated, we were devastated, the whole bloody country was devastated. We spent all of the next day in school talking about it. The nuns were all crying and we all said prayers, sang hymns and wrote in our copies about it as our 'News of Today'. I think the whole country went into shocked mourning.

To put it in context – imagine if something similar happened now to Barack Obama. Imagine the impact that would have on us all. All that great hope, energy, intelligence and vitality he has brought to the world, all being wiped out – well, that dreadful feeling you might have was the way we experienced it in the winter of 1963.

I started school in the local Convent of Mercy and I loved it. I loved two particular nuns: Sister Thomas, who taught us in Low and High Babies (now Junior and Senior Infants) and Sister Carmel who took over after Sister Thomas. Sister Thomas was sweet, gentle and kind, slow to slap and with a great devotion to the Blessed Virgin, which she passed on to every one of us in the class. She told us the most marvellous stories, all the usual children's fairy stories and some of the great Bible stories. Sister Carmel was older than Sister Thomas – but she too was gentle. She would have been the person to teach me 'joined-up' writing – my sister said recently that my writing now is eerily reminiscent of Sister Carmel's at that time, neat and flowing. Sister Carmel always got one pupil to carry in the copies and her books from the office to the classroom. I was carrying her books one day and one of them dropped. I saw the number '33' written on the flyleaf and later on I put my hand up in class.

"Yes, Eamon, what is it?" she asked.

"I know what age you are, Sister," I piped up.

"Do you now? And what age would that be, young man?" She smiled, so I knew I wasn't in trouble.

"Thirty-three, Sister . . . I saw it on your book!" Sister Carmel laughed and so did everyone in the class. I was delighted with myself.

Sister Thomas died – she was quite young when she died – and we were taken to the convent to see her laid out. I was scared and didn't want to go in, but Granny made me and afterwards I was glad because Sister

Thomas looked so peaceful that I knew death wasn't something to be scared of. It was like she had told us, a happy and peaceful place. The room was dimly lit and a tall candelabrum with six flickering candles stood beside the open coffin where she lay, her much-used rosary beads wrapped about her hands. She looked as she used to look when she was leading us in our prayers, as if she were in a trance. That had always amazed me, that look on her face when she prayed. I knew she went to another world when she was praying – somewhere safe – distant and safe. And she passed that safe place on to me and to all her pupils.

After the funeral Mass we came home and I went up to the gable room to pray, to think and to feel peaceful with the calm face of Mary and her beautifully draped simple clothing looking down on me. I thought about the soul of Sister Thomas now being with Our Lady for all eternity. I knew, just knew, that Our Lady loved me and would protect me. To this day, on my very worst days and in my darkest moments, that is where I go in my imagination – to that little gable room in the Corner House, that is long demolished, where Mary's serene face and open arms welcome, always welcome, me in.

2

The Last Days of Childhood

There was one day in school in 1965 that I remember particularly because I was raging. Rip-roaring mad and raging. Josephine Coyle, who was my best friend, had won 'Scholar of the Week'. That was the second week in a row she had pipped me at the post – it was usually one of us that got it. Josephine got first prize, a lovely holy picture of St Bernadette of Lourdes – and I only got a *milseán* for being second best (though normally I would have loved a sweet).

I was particularly annoyed because St Bernadette – Bernadette Soubirous of Lourdes – was my favourite saint. The last time I had won 'Scholar of the Week' it had been a Padre Pio picture the *múinteoir* had given me. I liked Padre Pio, he was a really good saint and all, but for me he wasn't a patch on St Bernadette. All the pictures and statues of Bernadette of Lourdes were beautiful – she had a soft, kind look in her eyes – and

21

the wonderful story of her life! I preferred her even to St Therese of Lisieux and she was beautiful too. I would imagine St Therese of Lisieux or St Bernadette of Lourdes appearing in Granard and thought that they would probably pick me as a best friend. Then Josephine Coyle would be mad! But I'd let her play with us too. I thought I would anyway, if she was nice to me, maybe.

Dixie, our dog, was waiting for me outside the school gate as always and I ran as fast as I could with him, away from the other children of my class, so they wouldn't see how annoyed I was. Dixie was great – he always came to meet me. I was relieved that at least it was also the day the comics arrived at the shop, so that was something to cheer me up. Everyone in Granard's National School was mad jealous of our family on comic day. As we owned the shop we got to read all the comics the day they came in. *All* of them – not just the one your mum bought you for a few pennies.

My favourite comic was the *Bunty*. Lucy always had her own copy but Granny held a secret Bunty aside for me because of the absolutely best thing about the *Bunty* – the back page. It had a picture of this Bunty character on it, standing with her arms and legs slightly apart, wearing just her underwear. There were also pictures of two outfits for Bunty on the page with little tabs on them at the shoulders and waist. You had to very, very carefully cut Bunty and the outfits out. Then you stuck Bunty and, separately, her outfits onto thin cardboard, and when the glue dried you cut all the excess bits off.

You could then 'dress' Bunty in whichever outfit and accessories you liked. You gradually built up a huge wardrobe of paper clothes for your paper doll.

Lucy would want her own Bunty dolls, hence the second copy for me. I had dozens of Buntys with dozens of outfits. I would line them all up on the sideboard and move them about, having little chats with each other, then maybe I'd have them dancing together. I staged fashion shows and all sorts of happy gatherings with my Buntys.

I did Irish dancing and I liked my Irish dancing costume: the kilt, the smart little jacket with the bright shiny buttons, the highly polished shoes, and the knee-high socks with the little ribbon on the side. I wanted – I really, really wanted – a girl's costume though. And those ringlets they got! It just wasn't fair.

One day I got into terrible trouble because I tried on Lucy's First Communion dress. It was in a neighbour's house. I don't know why Lucy's dress was there but I spotted it on a chair in a bedroom and I sneaked away from the children with whom I was playing and pulled the dress on over my shirt and shorts. Lucy had made her First Communion the previous year and, as there was no-one else in our family for it to be passed on to, perhaps it was being passed along for one of the neighbour's children. I remember feeling very excited when I put it on – excited and happy. It was miles too big for me – I was a little runt of a child and Lucy was fourteen months my senior – but I pulled it in around me and imagined what I could do with it to make it look better. I thought it was gorgeous, despite its size. I got caught though, by the mother of the house, and she scolded me and told me she was going to tell my gran. I was terrified going home that night. I thought I would be in the most awful trouble but my wise grandmother said nothing at all.

I can still remember the feeling of 'rightness' about wearing the dress. But I couldn't have expressed it. Boys did not wear dresses. Full stop.

When Lucy made her First Holy Communion I was jealous of her and all the girls, not because of the hansels they got to put in their new bags but for their beautiful white dresses, their diaphanous veils and their frilly ankle socks. I was raging. They looked like angels, and when my turn came, the following year, to make my Communion, I refused to wear the standard suit. I wheedled Granny into buying me snow-white, well-cut shorts and a dazzlingly white shirt and slipover, and I topped off the whole outfit with a royal-blue velvet dickey-bow and a divine royal-blue jacket with silver buttons. I was the Bee's Knees, the Cat's Whiskers. But it still wasn't the dress I knew I should be wearing.

It is hard looking back at the boy-child I was supposed to be in rural Ireland in the 60s, from this distance. The world is a completely different place now. I hope life for the next generation of third-gender people will not be as difficult as it has been for me. I knew from a very early stage, maybe from about three years of age that I was female, but it is only with the benefit of hindsight that I can say yes, yes, I always knew I had a female brain, heart, soul and psyche, but God got the packaging wrong and I got a male body – but I could never ever have articulated it or even thought of it in that way then. Conventional wisdom tells us a baby is either a boy who grows up to be a man or a girl who grows into a woman. However, reality is not always as simple and clear-cut as having only two possibilities.

Gender identity is fixed, immutable and irreversible by any known psychological means. There is only one way to determine anyone's gender identity: ask them. When I went to the bathroom then – even as a very small child – I always insisted on sitting. I never stood to pee. In public toilets I would always use a cubicle and sat to pee. But how can you tell people what you are if you don't have the words to know what you are?

I assumed all boys felt like me, thought like me. What else could I assume? Everyone kept telling me I was a boy, bought me boy toys and boy clothes. I tried very hard to conform, to behave as society and people about me expected me to behave. I tried to develop in a certain way, a way that was totally against all my natural instincts, a way in which it was almost impossible for me to develop and be happy. No wonder I got into trouble later in life, in school and in my teens.

At some stage in those early years I'm quite sure the adults about me did notice my 'being different' but nothing was ever said. For example, I loved Lucy's 'Sindy' dolls (a version of Barbie) and always played with them, changing their outfits etcetera. They must have known there was something different about me.

But there is a saying in rural Ireland: 'Well, sure – he's himself.' A catch-all phase to cover a multitude of differences. I assume they decided: if he's going to play with dolls it had better be a boy doll. So 'Action Man' was purchased. Boring – in his khaki and camouflage – until I discovered you could get other clothes for him. My Action Man got a makeover – he had a divine one-piece white leather jumpsuit! One day I dressed him in Sindy's clothes. He looked ridiculous and we all laughed. I wondered if I would look ridiculous in bigger Sindy clothes? I didn't think so. I was of slight build and had small feet. I thought I would look great.

I always loved chatting to people, and have always been emotional and cried easily. I was very, very aware of what was going on in the lives of those around me. I also think and tell stories in a circular feminine way, not a straightforward male linear statement of facts and figures. I hate generalising – but we all do it – and, 'in general', I think most people would see all of those traits as female traits, in the majority that is. I, more than most, am aware that one cannot pigeon hole people – no one size fits all – thank God too. Wouldn't the world be an extraordinarily dull place if we were all clones of each other?

Our home in Granard was a predominantly female house. As my father was gone before I was two years of age, all my early lessons in life came through women. There were uncles and other males about but I don't particularly remember them having any great influence on me. I do remember my Uncle Bill, Aunt Phyllis's husband, saying at some stage "that fella should be wearing a skirt". Bill was also one of the first members of my family who accepted my gender reassignment completely. I was still Eamon to him whatever clothes I wore. Bill was a lovely man. Whenever I think of Aunty Phyllis and him, I think of grapefruit. When myself and Michael stayed with them, he always cut a grapefruit in half and gave us half each, cut into easy-to-scoop-out sections and sprinkled with sugar! We thought it the height of sophistication. I really loved this family, but poor Aunty Phyl was often ill, and Bill and Cathy, their daughter, looked after her. I remain close to Cathy to this day.

I never had doubts about my gender and sexuality. I knew I was female. If I thought about it at all – which I tried not to – it would have been: *'I don't know why I feel this way. It's not natural.'* But then I would work out that if I did feel that way, and had been made by God through my parents, it had to be natural – didn't it?

I certainly knew after puberty that I was attracted to men. But any whispers I'd heard up to that point taught me to keep my mouth shut. I saw how 'queers' and 'nancy boys' were treated. Anyway, I wasn't that, or so I thought at that early age – I knew what I wasn't, I just wasn't sure what I was. But society and my religion conditioned me to think differently – to have doubts that the way I felt was 'right'. So I just didn't think about it. I pushed it away and just got on with day-to-day living. But when I was a kid, I was just Eamon and being Eamon meant I could only be what I was, female in a male body, not what everyone else said I was.

Society – school, church, home – all told me I was quite definitely one thing and I didn't know there were any alternatives. As a child and a teenager, or even as a young adult, being gay wasn't spoken about so I didn't know which side of the road to go to. In fact, I wouldn't have been consciously aware that there was another side to the road!

Back to that particular comic day in 1965. It was a beautiful day and we were all going to the Geraghtys' house in Abbylara for a tea party. There were three Geraghty children, all the same age as us, and we all got along really well. The Geraghtys' father was a solicitor so they would have been considered as 'well-set'. They had a tennis court. A tennis court! It had real grass, white lines and the net and everything! I thought I was in a palace. I felt that only very grand and sophisticated people had tennis courts. Everyone else in the area played GAA – if they played any sport – and I hated football and hurling. The Geraghtys were the nearest thing to royalty we had in the area as their mother was a niece of Kitty Kiernan and, because of this connection, the Geraghtys were admired and respected by the bulk of Granard's population.

That day of the tea party in Geraghtys' is the last truly wonderful memory I have of childhood. It was one of those soft-focus-haze days of love, family and friends. I can hear the *thwock* of the ball on the court as older people played tennis. I can see the little pink and yellow French Fancies (little melt-in-your-mouth cakes) laid out on a doily on a plate and smell the apple tarts fresh from the oven. We were allowed fizzy orange and crisps, and didn't even have to finish our dinners before we had them! We raced about the house playing hide-and-seek, then 'Mammys and Daddys', then 'Cowboys and Indians' and 'Batman and Robin'.

When we got tired of that we went up to the Geraghty children's bedroom and played fashion shows with the Buntys. No wonder I ended up in the business I'm in – I had a headstart on everyone else – my own agency at seven years of age! My brother and the two Geraghty boys played with soldiers and little Dinky cars.

I would love to turn back time and pick up that happy little boy and tell him that I knew he was a girl, that I was going to smooth his path through life, hold his hand and help him make the right decisions. Perhaps if I could I would be a different person today. But I don't think so. I think we have to trip and stumble, fumble and fall our way through life, finally finding our own paths to our places of peace and serenity.

I know it was very soon after this that we all took a trip up to Dublin. We were excited. I don't think we had been to Dublin before and it was a great jaunt for us. Dublin, to us, was a sort of magical place, this big, mysterious, exciting metropolis – like Gotham City without the baddies – where Mum went during the week. I can't remember how we got to Dublin, whether it was a bus or a taxi or in some relative's car. Perhaps

Aunty Maureen drove us up, because she was definitely with us. I can still see myself standing on Leinster Road in Rathmines and looking up at Rathmines Town Hall clock.

When we reached Aunty Sybil's house, I stood at the gate and pointed to the clock exclaiming, "Look, Aunty Maureen, the biggest watch in the world!", and she laughed and squeezed my shoulder.

We went into Aunty Sybil's house and we were playing in her living room with cousins. I knew something important was going on – there were lots of adults going in and out between the kitchen and the living room, voices being raised and then shushed. I remember thinking – secrets, they must be telling secrets.

Then we were told – and I must have panicked, because I just cannot recollect which person actually said the words: "Eamon and Michael will be staying in Dublin and they are going to a boarding school. Lucy will be going back to school in Granard."

Away! Away from Granny and our house and our little school! I'd heard of boarding school, of course, from the *Bunty* and books, but for some reason an image popped into my head, and I can still see it, still see that image with my seven-year-old inner eye – it's a boarded-up window, a whole building with boarded-up windows. To this day I don't understand that, but it is the image that has stayed with me through all the years.

Then my sister Lucy went berserk, screaming and shouting because my brother and I were being taken away – we would be together and she would be on her own. Up till then Aunty Maureen and Granny in Granard had been the women in our lives, and now we were to be taken away from them.

I suppose that was the first time in my life where everything changed. Everything had been the same for ages and as a kid I liked that. I think all kids do, don't they, knowing what's going to happen next? And then, *vroom* . . . everything changes, upside down, and you don't know what to do or what to say and you don't know what's coming next.

3

Suffer Little Children

I don't remember who dropped us over to the boarding
school, which it transpired was actually an institution
on the Northside of Dublin. I'm not even sure why that
place was picked. I don't remember asking why we had
to go and it wasn't until thirty years later that the reason
came to light. It wasn't Mum who dropped us at the
school, of that much I am sure, but I can't recollect the
person who did. I know it all happened on the same day
but it seemed as if it all happened in five minutes.

It must have taken hours. I mean, the whole packing
thing and getting us to the institution, which was on the
other side of the city to Rathmines where our relatives
lived. But for years it seemed to me as if we had been
teleported to the school, like we were just dropped out
of space into this big prefab room.

It was coming into evening and the room was dusky,
the only light from a small black-and-white TV in the

corner of the room, on a bracket halfway up the wall. I had never seen a television up high like that before. There were lots of chairs in the room, all facing the wall where the television was.

That's the memory, one minute being in Aunty Sybil's living room in Rathmines and the next minute in this big room with all the chairs. I suppose that's the way memory works. Only the strongest impressions remain.

Almost all the chairs were occupied. On each chair there was a child but we could only see the backs of their heads. They didn't turn to look at us and I felt scared. Brother Cecil (not his real name), who brought us into the room, turned on a little side light and it took me a minute or two to realise that the children were all boys. My heart sank – no girls to play with! I think the programme the children were watching was an Irish-made programme and for years I thought it was *Wanderly Wagon,* but it can't have been because that programme only started on RTÉ in 1967. It was a children's television programme anyway – and there weren't too many of them in 1965.

I thought it was very quiet for such a big room with so many boys in it. I was holding my brother's hand and we stood really close together. We could feel each other's fear. I had a bag of sweets and a Crunchie in my other hand – I could hear the paper on the Crunchie rustling. I suppose I was trembling. I can still feel that empty terror, that 'not knowing what's coming next' fear. It's the worst kind of fear really; the fear in a child who doesn't know what a new world is going to be like.

We weren't in that room for long. We sat for a while and watched television with all the other quiet boys. I was afraid to eat my sweets or open my Crunchie, in case it made a noise and they would all look at me. Brother Cecil left the room and then he came back in and took us by the hand and brought us across the yard to the Infirmary. This, apparently, was where the younger boys slept. The Infirmary was run by a matron; she was a little fat woman and she seemed nice. I could smell starch, from her uniform I suppose, and from the sheets on the beds. It was a smell I recognised and it comforted me a little – at least the place was clean.

There were about twenty small beds in the dormitory of the Infirmary. Twenty little steel beds, with tight neat grey blankets and a sheet turned over at the top, and a white pillow. It was all very uniform and no colour. Just grey and white, and the grey steel of the bed frames. Wall-to-wall beds. I do know that I didn't feel as scared when I saw the dormitory because the children there were all small like us or smaller. I suppose all of us were under the age of eight and I thought I'd be all right, if the kids were all about my age or younger.

One part of me was excited. I know children now frequently have sleepovers in each other's houses, lots of friends together. But I don't think it was a common thing in the mid-sixties in Ireland – it was a novelty for myself and Michael, barring a week in Courtown in the summer, we never slept anywhere except our own beds in the Corner House in Granard.

On that first night in the Infirmary, I watched my brother fall asleep before me. I tried to keep my eyes open to watch over him but they kept closing, no matter how hard I tried. When we woke up he was upset. I asked why and he showed me the wet yellow stain on the bed where he had wet it in his sleep. He was only six years of age; a baby. There were other boys standing by their beds and, from the looks on some of their faces, I thought there might have been other wet beds too. Michael was red in the face and almost crying, which made me want to cry too. I could see he was terrified – he had never wet the bed before this, or if he had I didn't know about it. It would have been hard enough if he had pissed the bed at home where he would be scolded by Granny or Mum. But here? In a room with dozens of others? Terrifying.

As little boys we looked very alike. I was the older brother, but I was a bit of a runt and not much bigger than him. I felt responsible for him, so I pulled him by his arm over to my bed and I stood by his bed and he stood by mine. It was worth it; I saw the fear and shame leave his face. I felt proud and brave – a big brother.

I think that was the first time that I came fully to the attention of Brother Cecil. In any big institution the best way to stay safe is to keep quiet, mind yourself, and under no circumstances draw attention to yourself.

Every night each one of the 'piss-the-beds' had to go up to the charge-hand for a tablet. I don't know what the tablet was but we were told if you took the tablet you wouldn't piss the bed. There probably wasn't anything in it, it was most likely a placebo, but we thought there was medicine in it and so it worked. I never wet the bed before or after so I don't know about its effectiveness. I don't think it ever happened to Michael again either – at any rate he never mentioned it again. We used to dread lining up for the tablet because the charge-hand was an older boy – to me he was an adult but I think he might have been fifteen or sixteen. He was mean and would rap us across the knuckles with the handle end of a big pair of tailor's scissors and we all feared him. There was no softness in that place. No softness or kindness anywhere.

We didn't stay long in the Infirmary, just a few weeks, and then we were moved over to the big house.

My brother was really good at hand-ball and there was a hand-ball alley where we played. I wasn't as good, but I was glad Michael was good and made friends with other boys who liked hand-ball too. One of the Brothers was mad about hand-ball and he was nice to any of the boys who showed promise at the game. I loved swimming and there was a pool in the institution which was fairly new at the time – it was open to the public at certain times and other times just for us. I thought this was a grand thing to have, just like the boarding schools in the *Bunty*. I loved jumping into it, everything clean and shiny and new, white tiles and blue, blue water. Michael was terrified of water and it was the one area in school where I was better than him. I loved diving in, disappearing under the water and then cutting through it in a steady front crawl.

I was five years in that grim grey place. Five long years. In at seven years of age – out at twelve, a life sentence at that age. It wasn't all bad – there were other kids and we did make fun for ourselves. We played games, laughed, were kids. We all liked Sunday mornings. It was porridge for breakfast every other day, but on Sundays we loved going down to the refectory because there was white bread and butter piled on plates for us to help ourselves from. We'd all queue up and we had it down to a fine art: we'd innocently place a slice as slowly as possible onto our plates and quickly slip another slice under the plate. Oliver Twist, eat your heart out!

I had Our Lady as a companion in the school too. I would pray to her that the Brothers would be nice to me and that I would be good. I was scared a lot and recently a psychiatrist pointed out to me how horrific it must have been for a child who was gender-confused to have been trapped, not only in a male body, but abandoned by family to an all-male institution. Our Lady was female, soft and kind, she would mind me, listen to me and I talked to her all the time.

As a child I never understood one particular thing about the school. There was a tuck-shop, and second-hand clothes were stored there too. We wore other people's clothes for the five years we were in that school. Why was that? We weren't poor and we assumed our mother was paying fees, so why did the Brothers put us in second-hand clothes? I can see it now of course. I was in an institution living on the charity of the Church, not in a proper *Bunty* boarding school. I was so fussy about clothes and I hated, hated, *hated* wearing ill-fitting worn clothing.

The abuse didn't start straight away. I know the first time I went up to Brother Cecil's room I didn't feel afraid, and those first few weeks I was afraid all the time. So it must have been after we settled in that it started. The physical and sexual abuse I received in this institution was meted out by two Christian Brothers. One, Brother Peter (not his real name) would simply stand behind me and rub his groin against me. I would feel him stiffening and then moaning. The other Brother, Brother Cecil, was more violent. Initially it was just groping at me. He would throw a thimble into my shorts and say: "Now I have to find that thimble!" and he would fondle my penis and groin and rub himself against me like the other fellow. But one day Brother Cecil buggered me before he found the thimble. He anally raped me. Buggered me until I bled, a trickle of watery blood running down the inside of my leg.

I distinctly remember that first time because it was just before Michael made his First Holy Communion and we went to visit all the aunts and uncles after the ceremonies. I was uneasy and couldn't sit still. I was too sore from being raped to sit for long and was agitated and fearful someone would find out and I would be in trouble. I think Aunty Sybil was the only one who noticed something was up with me as she watched me pacing about the house later: "Will you look at that fella? Walking the Seven Churches!" This was a saying of the time for anyone who paced about; I think it comes from the 'Seven Churches' pilgrimage in Rome.

When Brother Cecil was finished he would pull my shorts back up. He never said anything after he abused me, except for that the first time when he muttered I should go to Brother Peter for a towel. Brother Peter gave me a towel and I wiped my legs and bottom. Then he, Brother Peter, abused me too – in the way I already described. I thought him kind, imagine, because all he ever did was to rub his penis against my bottom. I remember I was so sore that day and I was really terrified someone would notice because then I would be in big trouble. I don't remember being told I had to keep it a secret or that I would be in trouble over it. There were never any words said. But in some part of me I knew it was secret, secret and wrong, because it felt wrong. It did not make me feel good, and nobody talked about it the way people talked about good things – like Christmas and birthdays and special days out. So I knew it must be a secret.

When Mum came up to the dormitory to get us before Michael's First Communion, I was half sitting on the edge of my bed, feeling ashamed and dreading meeting her eye. I felt sure Mum would know by looking at me what had happened. She was my mother. Mothers had eyes in the back of their heads – they always knew when you had been naughty, didn't they? I was afraid Mum would think me bold and not love me any more. I really felt guilty. I think that may have been the first time we saw Mum since we had started at the school and I was nervous the whole time. I was convinced that what had happened to me must be obvious to everyone from outside the school, everyone who knew me well – Mum and Granny, the aunties and my sister – they'd know something had been going on. I thought I looked different, I certainly felt different, and I avoided meeting any of their eyes all day. But nobody said anything or asked anything and so the day passed without incident.

For the first two years in the school we were only allowed home on Sundays. The thinking at the time was that this was less 'disruptive', both to the school and the family. Maybe they thought that the less younger children saw their families, the less likely they were to become upset on leaving them again. When we were older we were allowed home for the full weekend. Mum had a flat in Grove Park in Rathmines and Michael and myself walked across the city to it every Sunday during term-time. Sometimes we got a bus part of the way and walked the rest. We were no more than nine and ten but children had a lot more freedom and were given more responsibility then.

40

The abuse by the two men petered out after a few years, around the time of my Confirmation, I think. We made Confirmation when we were nine or ten back then and that's when they stopped abusing me. I knew they hadn't touched my brother because I had dropped hints and he hadn't any idea what I was talking about, so I stopped talking about it to him – I couldn't bear for anyone to know. I felt dirty. That is really the worst part of abuse, apart from the physical pain. It's how the abuser makes the abused feel. Bold and dirty.

Someone asked me recently when was the last time I was abused by either one of those men, and I remember the occasion vividly. My Aunty Phyl died and was buried on February 29th 1968 – it was a schoolday and I was delighted to get a day away from the place. Brother Cecil called me in to tell me I had to go home – then he buggered me, and we knelt and we prayed for my deceased aunt as my behind stung and tears ran down my face.

That was the last time he touched me. And do you know what the worst part of it all was? I missed it. I missed that special attention. No matter how painful, deviant and wrong their behavior was, at least someone was paying attention to me. I was special, different – at least that was how they made me feel – and now I felt dumped, just another one of the hundreds of little grey boys.

When the Brothers stopped sending for me, I thought I had done something wrong. I was actually quite upset because I thought they didn't love me any more. Is that terrible? I had been abused for almost three years on a regular basis and I thought they raped me because I was special and they loved me. That's how insecure I was. I even tried to get their attention again, keeping myself neat and tidy, making sure my shirt was buttoned properly and my shoes were shining, but they had moved on to younger prey.

There were older boys in the school, I don't know what age they were – they were fourteen or fifteen maybe – and they were allowed to smoke. There was actually a special room in the house set aside for these boys to smoke and hang about in. That sounds so mad now, in an Ireland where nobody can now smoke in any indoor public place, but in the late sixties, early seventies everyone smoked. It might as well be a thousand years ago, things have changed so much. Thank God for that. I remember wishing when I was about ten or eleven that I was older. Those boys seemed to be grown-up to me and to have so much freedom. They could choose to smoke and hang about with other lads, and not be as regimented as we younger boys were.

I became aware of one of the older boys noticing me, watching me in the same way as the Brothers had. I didn't avoid him. I didn't encourage him either, but I did know he noticed me. You do, don't you? That attraction, animal or otherwise, we are all very open to it – particularly when we're seeking love. It may sound terrible and I may do myself no favours but I have promised to tell the truth – my truth in this book. The truth is I was desperate for someone, anyone, to love me, hold me and be with me. Our Lady loved me, I knew, because I could sense her presence but I needed a physical love too, someone to kiss me, put their arms around me, be with me because they wanted to be.

One day I found myself alone with this boy in the toilets and he pulled me into a cubicle.

"We're going to do it," he said.

"I know how," I said. "You throw a thimble into my shorts and we can play 'hunt the thimble' – that's the way to do it."

We had no thimble but the older boy said we didn't need one, he knew what to do anyway. Then this older boy raped me. I was ten years of age, he was perhaps fourteen or fifteen. And he did so frequently over the next two years. I went along with it, thinking at least it meant he liked me.

When my brother and I finally left that school, I left with no regrets.

In my mind's eye I can still see that grey institutional building with its high walls and tall sash windows. It looked more like a prison than a school. If you look at primary schools now, you can see how we as a nation have done our best with the old buildings we were handed, brightened them up, made them as unimposing and fear-free as possible for our little ones. Thank God we are at least trying to leave the greyness and fear behind us.

43

But unfortunately times were more brutal then, the ruler and cane in full use – I'm glad all that has been left behind. There are indecent people everywhere, aren't there? People who hurt others simply to show their power or to gratify themselves with no thought for anyone but themselves. I don't understand how anyone – anyone – could hurt a child. When I look at the children in my life, at any time, I know that I would lay down my life for them. Our children civilise us, make us realise that every single one of us was once somebody's baby.

We must tell our children the truth, as much as they can handle, and as parents or loving guardians we will know what they can handle – they too will let us know how much information they need at the different stages of their lives. We cannot hurt our children with the truth. Trust yourself, trust them – tell the truth.

4

From Shamrock to Glam Rock

Looking back, I suppose it was a horrible childhood. As I said, I didn't know the real reason we had been sent to the institution – and would not discover that reason until 1997. None of us knows what goes on behind closed doors. Things are so well camouflaged, secrets and lies, secrets and lies, whispering and shushed voices if children come into a room.

From talking to friends of my generation I have discovered that this was a common theme in Irish family life of that era, perhaps family life worldwide. Keep the shiny, bright side forward, never let anyone know of the crap behind the curtains. We didn't have the knowledge, the education, the information or open access to same.

The Church practically ran the State and both institutions kept us in the dark, didn't they? That big slow-moving body of men with money – educated men, supposedly decent holy men – they kept the knowledge to themselves, didn't share it, treated us like silly children – only to be allowed to taste so much of life and what they considered bad for us was forbidden. But not to them. Oh no, not to the individual priests, brothers, men and women in power – it was all right for them to do as they did. We were children, we'd 'forget'.

We never forgot. It blighted our lives. I have never ever blamed Christ or God for my abuse. My religion is hugely important to me. I knew that what these 'men of God' did was nothing to do with Christ or real Christianity. Even then I knew that my faith and what were considered my duties in that faith were two completely different things. Perhaps it was the influence of the lovely Sister Thomas in Granard in my first two years in school – she was always so calm, so serene and holy. Perhaps it is simply that – Faith. I have fallen out with God on occasion, a sort of 'you made me this way, you let this happen to me' attitude. I never fell out with His Son Jesus or with Jesus' Beloved Mother. I always chatted away to them and they have brought me full circle – into this good space I now inhabit.

When Michael and I started secondary school Mum was still living in Grove Park in Rathmines on the south side of Dublin city, near to Aunty Sybil. I used to wonder why all our aunts and uncles had nice houses and Mum only had this horrible flat. With the innocence of a child, I didn't take into account the little matter of earning a living! I never liked that flat in Grove Park – it was small and poky and always felt crowded – I suppose, after the house in Granard, it quite simply didn't feel like home.

We did have good pals around Grove Park though. Children played out on the street in the 60s and, when we were allowed home – on Sundays at first and later on for the whole weekend, every weekend – Lucy would come up from Granny's house in Granard during school holidays and we would be freed from boarding school then.

I loved when we were all together. We were like the proper family we had been – the proper family I so desperately wanted again. We played out on the street with other local children and in other people's houses. I don't think many of the kids played indoors in the flat in Grove Park. Maybe they did – but it was a small place and it always felt transitory. Our playmates all had what we called 'real houses', family homes, full houses with gardens and all the usual playthings in their bedrooms, houses with stay-at-home mums, with dads who went off to work each day. Our flat was just the place we slept at weekends.

I was popular on the road, a bit of a ringleader, affectionately known by parents of pals as "a bit of a rascal". I had already started to move away from being the good little boy who tried to please everyone, at least in some respects. I had tried so hard to be good in Granard and I had been abruptly taken away from there, and being good in boarding school hadn't really got me far, had it? My schoolwork had already started to suffer by the time I was ten or eleven – actually, it is still something I am a little hung up about. I know I'm bright and I was certainly academic initially, willing to listen and learn both in the early years in Granard's National School and those first few years in the institution. Always anxious to please, to do well. Both my siblings were academic and they went on to do really well in exams and had great careers. At eleven or twelve I still had such 'potential' – as does every child of that age or at least one would like to hope so. Imagine, I never sat a state exam in my life! I have no educational certificates. I know this doesn't mean anything in the greater pattern of life etc, but it rankles with me. I could have, I should have done well in this area. Terenure College, where Michael and I started secondary school, was acknowledged as a school of academic excellence and was not unknown for its rugby – which I hated.

Despite this I was popular, and it was a time in my life that I particularly remember for feeling free. Incidentally, as I was thinking back to these times, I wondered why Michael and I ended up starting first year together, and remembered that I had been 'held back' in fourth class so we ended up in the same year. But for some reason neither Mum, nor any of the adults in my life were aware of that. They quite simply were never told. I couldn't imagine that happening now!

We were home every evening and at weekends so our little circle of friends grew. The kids in Grove Park went to Synge Street CBS or CBS Leeson Street. I actually don't know why Mum decided to send us to Terenure College in the first place. Maybe she thought it was a better school or perhaps she was already planning our next house move to Beechwood Avenue in Ranelagh. I don't remember exactly what year it was we moved, but I know I had been expelled from Terenure College before we moved to Beechwood Avenue.

We began mitching from secondary school very soon after we started there, I'm afraid. We would leave the flat, our schoolbags and uniforms on, but wait in the lane near the house and as soon as we saw Mum leaving for work we would head back to the flat where we held court! We would hang about all day, friends – both girls and fellas – dropping in and out during the day as they too mitched. I was full of devilment, mad for music and clothes and fun, fun, fun. The joys of early teenage years – no responsibilities, no intentions of ever having any and the only priority in any day being to have as much fun as possible! The complete restrictions of my primary 'education' and the freedom I now had sent me wild – wild with joy at being free, unfettered, unencumbered by any brooding evil waiting for me. I had a blast.

I have conflicting memories of this teenage period. They are strong memories but some appear contradictory and I have tortured myself trying to remember, 'Was that when I was fourteen or sixteen?' or whatever. I have tried for the most part to be accurate but my memories of dates, times and exact locations can be a little hazy. Forgive me if I make small errors in timing or detail.

I had a Saturday job in the city centre on-and-off for a few years in my early teens, in a clothes shop called Mr Gear in North Earl Street, so I had a few bob in my pocket. It seems so funny now, that I was going out to work at that age. It was paltry money, even for that time, but everyone's wages were incredibly low. I left most of my earnings behind me in the shop every week anyway – on a must-have shirt or a pair of flares. Elephant flares – can you picture them? I remember one of the days that Michael and I mitched we spent with two girls and we tore up the seams of a pair of bell-bottom jeans and hand-stitched in a flap of contrasting fabric. They were gorgeous – the height of fashion and original. My first piece of designer handmade *haute couture*! Clothes had become more unisex and girls and boys dressed alike a lot of the time: jeans, bell-bottom trousers, brightly coloured tops and shirts.

Eventually my absences caught up with me in school and I was expelled from Terenure College – mostly for mitching but also for bad behaviour and being a 'bad influence' on my brother. Poor old Michael, he was expelled too and Mum moved him to St Michael's in Ailesbury Road. I was supposed to go there also but I dug my heels in. I was incredibly stubborn about it. No way was I going on to do any more schooling. I just wanted out. Mum didn't put up too much of a fight; she knew I wasn't going to go back quietly. I could see I could earn a few pounds working and the less control any teacher or adult had over me the better. As far as I could see up to that stage in my life very little good had come of grown-ups being 'the boss of me'.

Someone asked me was I ever bullied in Terenure College, particularly because of my disinclination for sport in a rugby-playing school, and also because I was a runt until my late teens when I finally took a bit of a stretch. I can honestly say I didn't see any bullying in that school. I certainly wasn't bullied, but then I was very much my own person and able to stand up for myself. I suppose I was afraid of nothing, thought nothing worse than what had happened to me in boarding school could happen. Innocent, naïve, whatever you like to call it, but a rod of steel inside me – one that was to stand to me in later life.

So there I was, still out 'playing' on the road – and yet my education had finished. I was cast adrift in the world of adulthood and work and I was still a child. Lucy was in school in Granard and Michael was in St Michael's. It was a most fractured and brief childhood, but I didn't think about it like that at the time. It just was. It was my life.

Mum got me an apprenticeship at a French polishing and antique-restoring workshop, Edward Wrest's of Blackberry Lane. It was 1972 and I was fourteen.

I remember Aunty Sybil sighing and saying: "Well, it's a trade, I suppose. He'll not starve."

That song 'Clair' by Gilbert O'Sullivan was on the go at the time. I heard it every day on the radio in the workshop. I loved it, would sing along with it as I worked on a table or chair or whatever Teddy Wrest had me doing. I liked the work and it gave me a love of good furniture, nice pieces with that lovely deep sheen of old age and quality. I hated the standing all day though and at times the work was fairly monotonous and, as I was

51

a kid and a restless soul to boot, it's no real surprise that I didn't stay too long at it. I was always chafing at the bit, wanting to go on to the next thing, see what else was out there.

Around that time I was constantly plagued with a terrible pain in my side and Teddy sent me home on more than one occasion. Mum took me to a local doctor and he said I was "acting-up"; he couldn't find anything wrong with me. So Mum sent me back to work with a scolding. I think I did act up a lot around that time. Not any more than any normal teenager, but again I realise – with the benefit of hindsight and bloody expensive therapy – that I would have been looking for attention. That need to be noticed, to be loved, to be special.

But that particular day I wasn't 'acting-up' and I got really ill at work and Mum was sent for again. This time she took me to a different doctor in Sandford Road and he thought it might be my appendix. So I was rushed into hospital. Now, despite the fact that I was working fulltime, I was still regarded as a child and so was brought to Harcourt St. Children's Hospital. It was all a bit of a blur. My appendix had actually burst and I was on the brink of septicaemia. I was taken to theatre immediately and the appendix was removed. When I came to, I was in a ward with all smaller children. I was disgusted. I was earning a living, a grown-up in the eyes of the taxman and there I was – in a kid's hospital! I felt so lonely for Mum and Michael but didn't want any of my friends to visit because I thought they would tease me for being in with the children. But the thing I missed most was music. I didn't have a radio or my records to fill my head.

The ward also reminded me of boarding school and I was afraid a lot of the time, waiting around to be told what to do and not to do – it brought back that fear, that 'not knowing what was coming' feeling. Even those starchy hospital sheets reminded me of the sheets in the dormitories in the Infirmary. I couldn't wait to get home and, being a drama queen, declared it was the longest week of my life – I milked it for all it was worth.

But when I got home Mum put no pressure on me to return to work and all was quiet for a while.

This was shortly after the time we had moved to Beechwood Avenue in Ranelagh. I can still remember the excitement of that move. A whole house – just for us, the four of us. We ran in through the hall door that first day, small kids again as we ran around and around all those rooms, looking, calling out to each other to admire something or other, delighted with ourselves.

I always noticed little details – again a pointer to my creativity and how important the 'look of things' was going to be in my life. The tiles in the kitchen were unusual – they looked more like embossed wallpaper, very funky and 70s with figure-of-eight type of wavy lines, as opposed to the normal square tiles which were all I'd ever seen before. And there was a utility room – with a washing machine! I thought Mum must have come into money; before I went to boarding school I had only ever seen a twin tub for washing clothes. That was one unwieldy process! A day's work. First you filled one tub with water and detergent and the machine washed the clothes (an electrically powered centrifuge); then you drained the water and moved the clothes into the second tub where you rinsed them. When they were rinsed the wet clothing had to be fed into the red rubber rolls of a wringer. Granny must've had muscles of iron for she could rattle that wringer's handle like lightning and squeeze the water out of the wet fabric. None of us children could even turn the handle!

So there we were – obviously rich, in a whole house with a washing machine just for us! On the ground floor there was a living room, a laundry room and a dining room with French doors that opened onto the back garden where there was a swing. A fucking swing. I was in Heaven, a childhood I had been robbed of given back to me when I thought I was too old for such things. I loved that swing. You're never too old for a swing. The freedom of a swing when you're young is something else, isn't it? Legs out – head back – higher and higher, until you feel like you're flying and nothing or no one can catch you, pin you down, make you do stuff you don't want to do.

The house looked like a bungalow from the road but it had a lower level, a sort of basement. My bedroom, the kitchen and a small 'second' bathroom were in the basement. In Ireland of the early 70s, a second bathroom was the height of sophistication. There was a powder-blue shaggy carpet in that bathroom; Jesus, I loved that carpet! I would spend hours in the loo admiring myself and the shaggy carpet! I'd never even heard of shaggy carpet before that; in Grove Park there was linoleum and a Hessian-like carpeting called 'tintawn'. Both that loo and my bedroom were my bolt-holes in the house. From the top of the window in my bedroom the small front garden was at eye-level. I always felt really safe in that bedroom. I wonder why? Was it because it seemed to be hidden from the world? My own private little burrow.

So I was quite happy to recuperate in our nice new home after my appendectomy. I would spend the day on my own, playing records and listening to the radio. Music, music, music all the way and, as soon as my side mended, dancing, dancing, dancing, around the kitchen, the living room and in my bedroom. I was music mad and still am. I bought my first record when I was thirteen in January 1971, in Caroline's Records just over Portobello Bridge. It cost 7/6d – seven shillings and six old pence. It was "Yellow River" sung by the British band Christie. Doesn't that price look so funny – it looks old-fashioned – two currencies ago!

Music and dance has always played a huge part in my life. I was such a girl when it came to music! Donny Osmond and David Cassidy were the heart-throb pin-ups at the time for teenage girls. Oh God, I loved Donny Osmond! I had the most enormous crush on him – I'd imagine meeting him and him smiling at me with those dazzling straight white teeth. I'd be struck dumb with delight, then he would take my hand, look into my eyes and sing me a song – a special song written just for me that only he and I knew about. All those clean American kids, we loved them, their glamour, their wholesomeness. David Cassidy was a bit more rugged but still smooth in comparison to Irishmen. Teenage dreamboats. The 70s were a great time for what they called glam rock: Slade, T Rex, Sweet, Adam Ant. I loved Gary Glitter too. All showmen, flamboyant. I loved them all. Michael Jackson, myself and Donny were all born the same year and I always felt a secret affinity with them because of that. To this day I still fancy Donny Osmond!

When I stretched the 'recovering patient' as far as I possibly could, I went back to working in Mr Gear at weekends and other clothes shops around the city. It was all right – I didn't want to stay working in shops forever but it was less arduous than Teddy Wrest's. I was a bit of a monkey – I might do a few weeks in one shop then move onto another, all without telling Mum. Then she'd find out and there would be a row. I couldn't understand this. What did it matter to her where I worked? Typical teenage behaviour: 'Hello! This is my life what's it got to do with you?'

My cousin Mary suggested I try hairdressing, because I was always messing with her hair and the hair of all the girls in our group. They would ask me for advice about clothes and hair and make-up. They trusted my judgement. So I thought I would give it a go – but was determined it had to be a unisex salon. I didn't want to work in a barber's or a 'Ladies' Salon'. All those old men looking for short back and sides and talking about football! Or old women looking for sets and blue rinses and talking about knitting patterns – *Yeucch*!

So I was taken on as a junior hairdresser in His 'N' Hers – a salon in the city centre. Unisex hair salons weren't all that long in Dublin and male hairstylists were on the increase. But it was still mostly female hairdressers and I always felt more comfortable with women. I liked boys but in a different way – I couldn't relate to them. I wasn't interested in a lot of the things they were. I might say I fancied someone, a girl, but it was probably her clothes or better still (although not acknowledged by me at the time) her body. I wanted a girl all right but not in the same way a boy longs for one. But I wasn't to know that. I just thought other boys must 'fancy' girls in the same way.

I settled quickly into hairdressing and I liked the laugh I had with the other juniors. We were in awe of the stylists and I would closely watch what they were doing. Dying to get my hands on a pair of scissors and start sculpting! I realised that this might be something I could be good at. Maybe I'm a typical second child from that point of view: I never felt that I quite measured up – Lucy and Michael seemed to be best at everything, and Piggy-in-the-middle never did anything right. The family would nag me asking why I couldn't behave more like my siblings. Hello! I wasn't them. I was so confused all the time about everything, always this sense of longing for something but not knowing what that something was. Maybe hairdressing would be my 'thing'. Something I did better than anyone in the family. I also loved all the chat about hair and clothes and we juniors would experiment on each other. Mum could see I was finally making an effort at something and there were less rows at home. I thought I'd found my niche.

We made friends quickly in our new neighbourhood of Beechwood Avenue and the surrounding streets. Oh God! I still love that area so much! If I ever win the Lotto I will be walking up and down Beechwood Avenue looking for 'For Sale' signs. Our Grove Park friends were soon forgotten and our social lives definitely took an upswing. There was a large group of teenagers in the area at the time and we'd congregate on the corner. "Meet you at the corner!" was our mantra. All of 500 yards from each of our homes! When I came home from whatever job I was at and Michael came home from his school – St Michael's in Ailesbury Road – we would join them. We did what all teenagers do: preen, gossip, bitch, smoke fags, talk about music and how much we hated our parents etcetera, etcetera. These teenagers from our Avenue and from Dunville Ave, Oakley Road and other places were all good kids from nice homes.

I was in and out of hairdresser training over the next year or two, never settling long, but I did manage to finish my training. I would get fed up with one salon and leave and if there was a break between jobs I'd work in boutiques around the city. I'm sure the other children's parents would have looked at that and thought it odd. Middle class kids normally at least finished their secondary education. Only the poor or the 'common', as we in our middle class snobbishness thought of them, had to go out to work early. Maybe my friends' parents warned their teenage sons and daughters to steer clear of me, I freely admit I had a 'divil may care' attitude and was probably regarded as a bad influence.

Of course being that bit different only made me more exotic and attractive to teenagers desperate to be different from their parents. The girls all loved me – little did they know I was one of them! We were innocent enough when I look back now: we went to discos when we could afford it, hung around each other's houses chatting and playing music, dancing – making up our own routines to songs. The worst thing we did was one night we broke into an abandoned house on Beechwood Avenue and brought a Ouija board with us.

"Did it move?"

"It did – oh, janey!"

"It didn't! Eamon Tallon – you moved it."

"I did not. Look, it's happening again!"

We scared the lives out of ourselves and laughed and laughed and laughed.

That's what I remember most, the drama of teenage romances and laughing. I just put all doubts and worries out of my mind, surrounded myself with people who were fun and kept myself busy every minute of the day – that way I didn't have to think. I knew at a very deep level that something was wrong, but I couldn't put my finger on it. I still never told anyone about the abuse. It was there, though, and I would always be a bit uncomfortable if I was left alone with older men who weren't relatives. I'd try to find out how my friends felt about things; about kissing, fancying someone and being attracted to someone. I knew my feelings were different to theirs – but I don't think I ever articulated it.

Mum was never a woman who got to know her neighbours. She was always a little distant with other people, even children, partly because she was working all the hours she could, but also because she was a private person and didn't want others knowing too much about her. I think that can be the case, particularly when you come from a small community where not much happens and people do tend to watch each other. Not maliciously, just to keep informed in some way, or maybe people are just plain nosey! Anyway, Mum had Aunty Sybil nearby to keep her company and they were good pals, went shopping together, talked to each other – I'm glad Mum had someone she could talk to.

I was always very proud of my mum. She was always a very beautiful woman and looked after herself so well. As we were always going in and out of friends' houses you'd get to know their mums and dads, but my mum always held herself apart from that. She was always polite but distant with our friends. She had her own reasons, I'm sure. Perhaps she felt different or embarrassed because she was a separated parent. It sounds mad even saying that now, but society in Ireland then was a world away from the modern inclusive society in Ireland today.

I don't think I ever had a birthday party as a child. There would have been a cake produced all right and candles but I don't ever remember a big deal being made of it, people being invited and bringing cards and presents and playing games. My cousin Mary, who lived in Grove Park, had a party every year on January 16th and it was a big deal in our family. We all would count down the days to Mary's party from Christmas on. It was the next big 'thing' in our lives. Her parents always threw her the best parties. Proper parties with games, music and party food. I'd see all of Mary's presents and I suppose I was envious, but not in a bad way, sort of sad really – not for the stuff itself but for the symbol of affection that the stuff was. People loved Mary so they bought her presents to celebrate her birthday with her. That's the way a kid's mind works, isn't it?

Mary has played a big part in my life and has always been supportive of me – even when I was at my worst. We were great pals and still are. Mary was the youngest of Aunt Sybil and Uncle Jack's children – there was a big gap between her and her older siblings so she was much doted on. It didn't spoil her – she has a lovely sweet nature to this day. I always loved Mary's shoes and for ages her feet were the same size as mine and I'd always fit her shoes on when I was over there and admire the look of my feet in them. Until my feet eventually grew slightly bigger than hers and Aunty Sybil scolded me: "God Almighty, Eamon – will ye leave Mary's shoes be? You'll stretch them on her!"

Until I was thirteen or fourteen I always went home to Granard for holidays, Christmas, Easter and even mid-terms. Until I was about ten we always went to stay in the Corner House with Granny, but then she got too frail and ill and Aunty Maureen took over her role. I loved Granny and Aunty Maureen, really loved them.

Granny died – I think it was in 1972. I was fourteen and it was the first death I had been close to and I found the whole thing really morbid.

Myself, Mary, Michael and Lucy were all upstairs in what was called 'the hill room'– the room furthest up the hill of the Corner House – and we could hear all the prayers and mumbling from downstairs. Directly over the shop – which took up most of the ground floor (barring a small kitchen, bathroom and scullery) – was the living room of the house. This had become a bedroom for Granny as she had aged and become ill, and it was in this room she was waked.

Upstairs we were all messing, feeling hyper. Lucy was fifteen at the time but she was jumping up and down on the bed like a kid and her nightie flew up and I could see a darkness under her panties and I actually screamed, "What's that?!" She pulled her nightdress tight around herself: "Oh, it's just a bruise." And I accepted and forgot about it. I think I was fourteen, but that is how innocent we Irish kids were! It seems unbelieveable now.

It was the end of an era for the family. Granny had definitely been the dominant figure in our lives. After Granny died, Lucy went to live with Aunty Maureen and Uncle Pat. She had actually been living with them but would have been up and down to Gran a lot – looking after Gran in a way, which is a big burden on any young teenage girl. I really admire Lucy for all she did for Gran in her later years.

There is a family story that rumbles around from time to time that not long before Granny died two of Mum's brothers, my uncles, paid Granny a visit, and to get rid of Lucy they paid her a fiver to go down to Aunty Maureen for the evening, so they could 'chat' to Granny in private. Apparently they had already arranged for a local solicitor to call to Granny's house and they wanted Gran to change her will without witnesses other than themselves. Up to that, my family had always been under the impression that anything that was left – land, houses, money in the bank etcetera – would be going to Mum. I suppose Gran felt that Mum needed more help than the rest of her children.

I'm sure Mum was annoyed when everything went to my uncles and there was some tight-lipped, barely concealed annoyance in the faces of a few family members about that time. It can't have made things easy for Mum – she was still working and renting accommodation in Dublin and the rest of the family, barring Uncle Tom, all had places of their own. But Mum got on with it, as we all do.

I was a teenager, aware of it but it passed over me. A bit of gossip. Nothing else.

Lucy stayed in Granard until her Inter Cert (now Junior Cert) and then Mum moved her to Loreto on the Green. Lucy couldn't settle though so she ended up going back to Granard to finish her schooling. But she came up to Dublin for holidays and some weekends she would be home and we would all head into the city, to the Dandelion Market, Grafton Street and St Stephen's Green. It was all so cosmopolitan to us, seemed so urbane and sophisticated after the quietness of a rural childhood, then the greyness and the fear of institutional life in a boarding school.

I remember in particular one Saturday in 1974. I would have been almost sixteen and, although I was training in hairdressing I was 'between jobs' at the time, so I was doing the odd shift in Mr Gear. I was due in the shop that Saturday but I wasn't always the most diligent of employees and I had decided to give it a miss. I was in town, though I can't remember where I was going – probably to meet friends. It was May 17th, a Holy Communion Day. I was walking up O'Connell Street and I was particularly admiring the little girls in their finery, thinking back to trying on Lucy's Communion dress and the trouble I'd gotten into. I felt so grown-up and they were still just these innocent little kids.

Then it felt like the end of the world because I swear

the ground shook and the very air seemed to move as I heard the loudest noise that I had ever heard. A big explosion. A bomb had gone off in a parked car in Talbot Street. I will never forget the looks of horror on everyone's face and I'm sure my own face looked the same. Total disbelief. A bomb! In Dublin! On the street above the street where Mr Gear was, I saw a woman with blood streaming down her face, screaming and running into O'Connell Street and the look in her eyes – it was awful, awful. I remember being terrified to go back to work after that, into any of the salons or shops in the city centre. I decided I would hide somewhere in the house in the coming days – I was supposed to be working and Mum would think I'd gone. I'd seen the blood, felt the shaking ground, heard the noise and experienced the terror, and it was all I could think of. I was convinced that there would be more trouble.

I think that it was around this time that Mum came home from work one day, it must have been a weekend because Lucy was up from Granard, and said: "Now, I've something to tell you all. It's up to yourselves and I'm not putting any pressure on you. Your father has turned up again in Granard and he'd like to see all of you."

None of us said anything for a minute. A father! None of us really remembered a father in our lives. It had always been Mum and Granny and the aunties – the uncles were quieter and back then men weren't as involved with kids as they are now. So we talked between ourselves and we decided we would go and see him just this once. I suppose I had some romantic notion of Mum and him getting together again, even though she told us she wouldn't be coming with us, that she wanted nothing to do with him.

So off we went on the train and I remember the train pulling into Edgeworthstown Station where we were to meet my father, and looking out the window trying to spot him. I was, still am, a complete and utter romantic and I had a picture of a Clark Gable type in my mind and I imagined he would be strong and silent and his eyes would be full of tears when he saw us. I had visions of myself running along the platform to this man (in slow motion black-and-white, of course – sort of *Brief Encounter*!). I was in for a rude awakening.

There were two men on the platform and I thought: Who the hell do I run to?

Then one of the men stepped forward and stuck his hand out. I was horrified. He didn't have a tooth in his head and he wasn't the best-looking character. He was certainly no Clark Gable! I remember very little about the meeting; what we talked about or how I felt about him at the time. I remember being disappointed in him. I felt he didn't care about us, could never have as he had walked away from us without a backward glance.

The man who brought my father to the station drove us all back to Phil Smyth's pub in Granard. I found the smell of stale beer and fags was sickening. I think that might have been one of the things that turned me off drink at that stage. I was quite finicky about smells and things. So Dad bought Lucy and Michael a drink (even though Michael was only fifteen) and asked me what I wanted. I said I'd have a Britvic Orange.

"Have an effin' drink," he said. "You're no son of mine if you can't handle a proper drink!"

He was almost a caricature of the rural Irish male. The only thing I took from that meeting was him growling that I looked too much like my "c**ting mother". He didn't make too much of an effort to endear himself to us and I wrote him off as a dad after that. He came back to Dublin with us on the train and he stayed for a while with Aunty Sybil and Uncle Jack in Grove Park. Uncle Jack was delighted – he always got on with my Dad. As we were living in Ranelagh we didn't see too much of him. I do remember thinking that there was a lot of drinking going on amongst the adults at that time. Mum wasn't involved in that – she was working and had no wish to spend any time with my father. She wasn't a big drinker either.

The one thing I do remember is Dad's hands. They fascinated me – shovels of hands they were and yet he was capable of the most delicate of work. If you saw these paws you might assume him to be a clumsy man, but I remember him taking apart a tiny ladies watch in Aunty Sybil's kitchen and fixing whatever was wrong with it, then putting it back together again. "Fair play to you, Brendan, you could always fix anything mechanical!" Aunty Sybil said. He fixed the big grandfather clock in her hallway too and the musical chimes in her jewellery box.

One evening I was in Aunt Sybil's house when Mum arrived at the front door and Dad, half-jarred, was standing in the hall saying: "Come on in, Tessie. Come on in and have a drink. Sure it's all over now."

Mum didn't come in and I still don't know for sure what he meant by that. I could speculate about it. But that's all it would be: speculation. I do think Dad broke Mum's heart, that she really loved him. His walking away, leaving her with three children in a small town where gossip could tear you apart, and in a wider society that was judgemental and unforgiving. I admire her that she still held her head up – no matter what. I know he would have found it tough marrying into Mum's family. There is a strong matriarchal line in that family and each woman in it is tougher than the next. He obviously couldn't match up to Granny's expectations of what a man should be and she wouldn't have been slow to let him know that.

5

Salad Days

Okay. Gender. Sexuality. Where do I start? Where do any of us?

I was pubescent and experimenting, kissing and cuddling etc. As teenagers we are all round pegs in square holes or vice versa. It has to be the most confusing time of one's life, that wailing, "What's wrong with me?" And attitude of, 'What's wrong with the rest of the world?' I was a boy in his early teens in 1970s Ireland – therefore I 'went with' girls – at that stage I wouldn't have thought there was an alternative. My only experience of sex for a long time was the sexual intercourse forced on me in by those into whose care I had been entrusted. I didn't know what that was, not then. It was the older boy who later abused me who told me it was called sex. It had nothing to do with love anyway – so it wasn't that that I wanted.

When I was a teenage boy and 'getting off' (our term

for kissing, then!) with girls, I would have felt (I think) like I was pretending to be a lesbian: a woman getting off with another woman but without the sexual attraction that lesbians have for each other. I knew it felt off, wrong, not right, but I didn't know how I was supposed to feel. I think I just thought: *Well, maybe I just don't really fancy her.*

I envy young people today, with open access to all sorts of information, and guidance if they feel they are that bit different to 'the norm'. The main difficulty was that I didn't know 'how' or 'what' I was meant to feel. I accept that nobody does know in early teens but, as I listened to my pals and workmates talking about fancying a particular girl or boy, I knew I didn't fit into either category. I was attracted to boys, safe boys – like Donny Osmond – ones I could have a crush on, but I preferred to be with girls. I think. It all seems so far away now. Another life.

I look back at my teenage self and I cry. I wish I could show that Eamon the beautiful strong woman he would become and tell him it would be okay, help him not make so many horrendous mistakes. But I can't – so Eamon did all the kissing, cuddling and chatting up. I decided I'd work at it – continue to search until I found 'The One', everything would come right. I was, still am, an incurable romantic. I thought I would find the right girl and would love her the way a man loves a woman. Then I would feel like everyone else did. Maybe because I'm a Gemini and a good actress I managed to pull it off. Girls loved me, loved being around me. I suppose they sensed the femininity in me and were drawn towards it. I have always been able to re-invent myself, morph from one life to another, though sometimes not as successfully as others.

I thought I was brilliant, shining, invincible – if one can't feel that at that young age then one never will. I loved hairdressing and all my workmates were brilliant. I realised that I had found a sort of niche for myself. All the young men and women that worked there all dressed to impress each other every day. The 'fashion police' had nothing on us, for appearance was paramount to all of us and we watched each other like hawks to see who was the trendiest. The hairstyle of the time was that kind of ruffled gypsy look – that's what we called it anyway – I have no idea why. I never saw a gypsy with layered hair turned under like that either then or now!

I dyed my own hair flaming red at one stage and I looked like David Bowie. I loved the look of that man. It was mad! I loved it, not so much the actual hairdressing 'job' because I hated standing all day and most of the hair 'do's' were boring once I had mastered them – which was quickly, as my eye and innate ability to cut were generally unerring from almost the first time I picked a scissors up. It was the freedom the job gave me, a license to wear the clothes I wanted – mad shoes – and to do anything I liked with my hair. Hair is such a statement when you are in your teens, more than anything else it is what marks you as different from the previous generation.

The money was crap. But everyone's money was crap

in the 70s. Particularly when you were training. I think I got about £1.50 a week – that's less than € 2! At the time a pair of new shoes cost about three quid! There was one pair I coveted that was around that price. They were black patent women's shoes with a chunky wedged heel and I could see my face in them. I had to have them. My feet being small; they fit me perfectly. I'm five foot ten inches now but then I was only about five foot seven and my feet were always small for my height. Anyway, my foot never grew above a size six. Isn't that another pointer to a possible gender error, particularly for any medium-height Irish male? So I borrowed the money and spent two weeks' wages on the shoes. That wasn't the only time I spent more than I earned on clothes or shoes either.

In 1975, I was nominated for, and won, 'Young Hairdresser of the Year'. I can't remember who nominated me – it must have been the manager of His 'N' Hers. The Irish Hairdressing Federation ran the competition and it was sponsored by L'Oreal. Most of the salons were members of the Federation and the competition became a much bigger deal in later years. I had to go through a number of heats and then the final was on in the Green Isle Hotel on the Naas Road. I was nerve-wracked – until I started to style of course. Then I could lose myself in the work. I think all creative people tend to be like that. But it was hard to go back to the mundanity of being on my feet all day putting rollers in, the daily slog in a hairdresser's. It gave me a taste for the limelight that stood to me later when I was doing hair for fashion-shoots or celebrity events!

I was a brilliant hairdresser and I loved the creative part of the work. In 1975, I thought 'this is it'– I'm famous now and I'm going to be a millionaire before I'm twenty-one. Of course I wasn't.

About that time we used to go dancing to the Leinster Cricket Club in Rathmines. A big happy gang of us with all the usual attendant teenage scandals, heartbreak and angst. I met my first girlfriend there, my Lorraine. I still think of her; I have such good happy memories of her. Lorraine was a really pretty girl and she was quite shy and that was what attracted me to her – that inner quietness. We both enjoyed me doing her hair and I would advise her on clothes. She was happy for me to do that and that made me feel good because entrusting the way you look to someone else is a big thing.

Lorraine was from Blackpitts on South Circular Road. I can still feel her hand in mine as I walked her home up Grove Park to her house on the South Circular. We grew together, thought we were *the* young socialite couple in Dublin. Posh and Becks! Such innocence. Lorraine had a strong Dublin accent, at least to my Longford ear and my family – in fact a lot of rural families were the same – had a thing against people with what we called a working-class Dublin accent. But Lorraine won everyone around, even the toughest of my relatives because she was so beautiful and had such a lovely nature. She was a quiet, gentle girl.

When I got my hands on this quiet, little girl I turned her into an absolutely stunningly beautiful woman. She went from shy, little girl to Farah Fawcett-Majors under my tutelage. *Charlie's Angels* (the original!) was all the rage at the time and every girl who was interested in fashion had one of the Angel hairstyles. So I bleached and cut, blowdried and hairsprayed until Lorraine had a mane of hair any starlet would have killed for. We were 'together' from the age of about sixteen, and after I had groomed her I took her up to Grace O'Shaughnessy Model Agency – I had no fear or shyness in this area – and she got work! Oh Lord, we were so happy! Lorraine got a job in Barbarella's nightclub as a hostess; I can still picture her in this gorgeous red dress with a side slit, her hair divine (done by *moi*!), and a little tray that she wandered around with. She was really incredibly graceful and beautiful.

I was working on-and-off at PR in Barbarella's and other clubs. I went out every night filling my head with noise, music, people – anything to avoid facing myself and my 'problem'. I was in the clubs so often socialising that I got to know the management and made contacts with media people. Pirate radio stations were starting up around Dublin at the time and 'the youth' were challenging the establishment of RTÉ, which we felt was still stuck somewhere in the earlier years of the century; it certainly had nothing to say to us, we thought. I worked on the pirate radio station, Big D, along with Gerry Ryan and Dave Fanning. I'd organise dance competitions in the clubs, then advertise them with leaflets and little cards. I walked around all the pubs in the city promoting both the radio station, the clubs and the competitions in them. I was a flittering, fluttering creature, running from one job to another, often with a salon job by day and a job in one of the nightclubs by night. I can see now how I filled my days and nights, with work and people and clubs, anything and everything to prevent myself from looking into myself, deep into myself, and confront the truth that was there.

Lorraine and I moved on to the ripe old age of seventeen together – we thought we owned the world. I know I always felt safe with Lorraine, comfortable, and I told myself that this was love, that I wasn't a freak. God knew what he was doing and he had sent Lorraine to me to make sure I would do the right thing. I worked any hours I could at other things to reduce the number of hours I had to hairdress. It's mad: I love the creativity of hairdressing – on one head – but not the hundred heads with all the small talk one had to make. I was seventeen and only interested in clothes, music, myself and my friends. I got so bored so quickly of everything outside of that.

As I said, I did flit from hairdresser to hairdresser around Dublin city, but that wasn't unusual then. Lots of hairdressers moved around, looking for something different, different clients, a bit of adventure. Clients would often follow a stylist from salon to salon. Dublin was really only a big small town then (still is!) and all the better salons were located in the city centre within walking distance of each other. I think I worked in His 'N' Hers for four different periods back then and I also spent various periods in every Peter Marks (a large chain of hairdressing salons) in Dublin. Mum would get annoyed with me over changing jobs all the time – there were no mobile phones then and she might ring a salon looking for me, only to be told I had left a couple of weeks earlier and was working somewhere else. I would think I had told her and not mentioned it after that. It drove her mad and we would get into arguments over it.

"You'll never settle," she'd say. "Employers will get fed up and stop taking you on."

I can see now where she was coming from but at the time I just laughed. I thought I was brilliant, unbeatable. Christ, I wasn't yet twenty – I was immortal!

I know I fell out with Mum about this time but for the life of me I can't think which little thing was the trigger to my leaving home. She was probably nagging me for my flitting around jobs or for staying out mad late. One night I was ironing a shirt to go out and she sat in the armchair looking at me, arms folded and her legs crossed, the upper leg moving quickly up and down. I knew she was annoyed.

"You know," she said, "I think you are the only person I know who starts getting ready for going out at ten o'clock at night."

I wonder why that annoyed her? Did she envy me the freedom she saw I had? I've always been a night owl. I don't do mornings but I will quite happily potter about until the early hours of every morning.

In the summer of 1976, we were living in Palmerstown Road. We were always moving houses or apartments, and I was fed up with that too. I was almost eighteen and thought I was grown-up and should answer to no-one. I informed Mum, in the middle of another row, that I was returning home to Granard to live and that I'd get some sort of a job down there. Mum called a family powwow, and I was told I could not stay with Aunty Maureen and there was no work or home for me in Granard. The family decided that I was to stay in Dublin and make the best of it. Stick to a job, not stay out half the night and sleep the next morning away. Granny was long dead at this stage and Uncle Tom was living in the Corner House.

Uncle Tom was the only one in Mum's family who hadn't married and he took over the house when Granny died. He was, to put it kindly, slightly eccentric. He had the most irritating tendency of starting some project enthusiastically and then getting fed up and abandoning it. For example: he started to paint the hall door one day – did three quarters of it and then just stopped. I don't think he even noticed it was never finished – ever – till the day he left that house it stayed like that. So the house fell into disrepair. It was eventually bought by the County Council and demolished to widen the road. That really saddened me. I do have good solid memories of that house.

Uncle Tom had been staying with us the time of that 'family conference' about this wild child Eamon, and when he was leaving he said to Mum: "I'm off, Tessie. Away to Granard."

"Uncle Tom, can I go with you? Auntie Maureen won't let me stay with her," I pouted.

"Course you can, boyo. Fuck them, sure they're as odd as bejaysus!'

The phrase 'kettle calling pot black', comes to mind!

However, he did offer to put me up and I had a bag packed in two minutes flat – while Mum scolded Tom and he laughed at her.

We got into the little brown Fiat he had and rattled – and I mean rattled – all the way to Granard. He was the most reckless driver, sober or drunk, that I have ever come across. We came around a tight little bend in Castlepollard and I swear we were on the wrong side of the road and a car was coming towards us. I shut my eyes, screeched and started saying the 'Hail Mary'. This was it, I was going to die. But Uncle Tom just ploughed on and the other poor motorist had to drive into the ditch.

"Jesus, Uncle Tom!" I exclaimed.

"Fuck him! Why should I get out of the way for that fucker?!" And he had this self-satisfied grin on his face. Mad! Mad, mad, mad!

We hit the road in spots for the rest of the journey but arrived safely in Granard, pulling into the yard of the Corner House. The last time I had been in the house it had been home. But the home that Granny had tended with such pride had descended, quite quickly, into a midden – it broke my heart to see it like that; bits and pieces of jobs half-done, it was dirty, the house unloved, uncared for, both outside and in. I felt like crying.

Tom said I could sleep in the gable room and I was delighted for this was my favourite room in the house;

my special room, my bolthole. But now the room was dusty, unloved, even unfurnished. My favourite statue was gone, the nets I used to drape over my head as I prayed and dreamed, gone, the window naked. There was a camp bed in the middle of the room and that was all. I have no idea what he did with the furniture in the house. I know some of the aunts and uncles had picked favourite pieces to keep, but my God! The house really looked like an abandoned building.

I headed up the town to see if there was anything going on and I met John Stokes, a local lad around my own age. I told him my tale of woe. He could see I was really upset, and he obviously went up and told his mam because next thing I was invited to stay with them.

In summer 1976, I was eighteen and most eighteen-year-olds are mature young adults at that stage – or at least heading that way. But in retrospect I can see how I was still thinking and behaving like a thirteen/fourteen-year-old. For example, I had begged Mum and been given a Chopper bike for my eighteenth birthday in June. This was a bike that anyone, between the ages of ten and fourteen, coveted. It was kind of the PS3 or the Xbox 360 of the late 70s! Psychologists have assured me that this type of childish behaviour is quite common in the victims of sexual abuse. It was an attempt to reclaim the childhood I'd lost through abuse and being handed from Billy to Jack. My emotional growth had been stunted by early sexualisation. I know the adults in my life felt at the time that they were doing their best, but I think because of the abuse I was needier than most kids, and that emotional need wasn't met so I remained childlike emotionally. In fact, it is only in recent years that I have grown up in that area.

But I wasn't aware of my immaturity in Granard that day in 1976. Right, I thought. I don't need Mum, Maureen, Pat, not even Tom. I'm eighteen, a man, all grown-up.

I moved into the Stokes family home in one of the terrace of Council houses, just off Granard's Main Street. They were a sprawling, big, happy family who didn't have two ha'pennies to rub together but had a busy, busy home with people always coming and going and all waifs and strays welcome. They loved me and I them and I think of them with great fondness.

My family immediately put pressure on the Stokes family to make me go home to Mum. The Stokes would try to avoid any of my relatives when they were out and about – almost impossible in a town the size of Granard.

"Don't make me go back," I'd plead to Ma and Da Stokes. "Just let me stay awhile." They promised I could stay as long as I wanted. The only problem they had was that most of the male members of their family were unemployed and had to sign on at the Labour Exchange on a weekly basis in order to collect their unemployment benefits. Now, as I mentioned earlier my Aunty Maureen and Uncle Pat ran the local Dole Office and, when the Stokeses went to collect their benefits, my relatives would give them a tongue-lashing and beg them to send me back to Mum in Dublin.

"Don't be encouraging that fella's wildness – put him out on the street and he'll have to go home." That was what the lads heard every time they went into the office to collect their Dole. Then they would come home and tell me all about it and we would have a great laugh.

I spent a good few weeks with the Stokeses, hanging about, playing cards and laughing. That summer of 1976 was a really, really good one – brilliant. Probably the fact that I was free all the time would have had something to do with that. I actually don't think there has been a hotter summer in Ireland since. Any day we could we would head off to Lough Gowna. I actually clocked it on the car recently and it was almost four miles, but we half walked it, shirtless, bell-bottomed and in totally unsuitable shoes. We hitched lifts on donkeys and carts or tractors pulling trailers heading out to the bog – let me tell you the tan you get anywhere in Ireland where there is a bog nearby is unreal – a deep, deep glowing tan – St Tropez, eat your heart out! Sometimes one or two of the gang would have bikes and we'd go out two on a bike and then one would pedal back for the next hanger-on! We'd spend the day messing about in the water at Gowna – it almost dried up the weather was so dry and hot. We sunbathed, yapped* and generally larked about. It was very, very innocent fun and no thoughts of what I was or wasn't entered my head. Unless I was on my own. And it was almost impossible to be on your own in the Stokeses' house.

The only thing I missed about Dublin at that time was my Chopper bike because I was constantly depending on crossbar rides, hitches or that four-mile walk to the lake. Anyway, in August 1976, I asked Da Stokes could I go with him when he was driving to Dublin in his van one day. He had some business to do there and I planned to get into the house while Mum was working and collect the bike and some clothes. Da Stokes agreed to pick me up at the corner of Palmerston Road. I can see myself still, sitting on my Chopper, bag at my feet, looking up and down the road, wondering where he was.

He never turned up. I learned years later from one of his children that he had finally agreed with my family that my place was in Dublin. I'm sure my presence in his house was causing him a lot of hassle in the town. Anyway, he told them he would drop me back to Dublin, so my asking him for a lift to collect the bike was a way out for him. I was hurt, really hurt at the time because I had thought they really liked me – my old trick of looking for a family, any family. They did like me, but they weren't my family and God knows they had enough bother of their own without another wayward lad hanging about!

So Mum and I agreed on a truce and, after my layabout sunny summer, I set about looking for another job and life became quiet . . . for a little while.

6

Love and Marriage

I never seemed to hold a job down for long, always doing a million different things, earning a few pounds here and a few pounds there. I wonder now where I got all that energy from? It doesn't matter really – I had to be on the go, buzz, buzz, buzz – that way I didn't have to listen to my little inner voice – the voice that told me the truth, that particular internal monologue I drowned out with people, work, music, and eventually with sex, drugs, drink.

I'm sure I drove employers mad because I would flit from job to job, but I don't think anyone in the industry would disagree when I say I have almost a genius when it comes to creating 'a look'. I love creating new styles, finding exactly the right style that says what the client wants it to say and, like a lot of creative people, I'm a perfectionist when it comes to my discipline. My work is hugely important to me. But I was probably an employer's nightmare, because I am a free spirit and mundanity and rules have never been first nature to me. All the practising you have to do as an apprentice drove me insane – the art has to be in you, it must be innate; no amount of practice will make a stylist out of a barber.

As I said before, I love to dance and in the late 70s there was a huge interest in dancing competitions and they were all the rage in all the city-centre clubs. As often as I could I got decked out in all my finery and did the clubs with my friends. Sloopy's, Zhivago's, Barbarella's – we entered all their dancing competitions and had a ball. We would spend hours devising routines and go through them until we were happy we were great. I didn't drink – I had no interest in alcohol; it got in the way of the dancing and it made you fat! So it wasn't for me. *Saturday Night Fever* was the big movie hit about that time and *Grease* shortly afterwards. I think *Saturday Night Fever* reflected club-life in the city fairly well, even though it was set in the States. I was in my element; the white suit, shiny shoes and carefully slicked back hair. I got a job as a male 'go-go' dancer. People always seem to think that only women do this job and that it's akin to stripping, but it was perfectly harmless fun with no sexual undertones to it. The DJs and management of the clubs would keep an eye on the crowd and would approach the best dancers male and female to see if they wanted to dance alone on various podiums positioned about the club. We would do half an hour on the podium and half an hour off. The limelight never bothered me. I was quite happy to be above the moving crowd dancing on my own, my head full of disco music. I got paid for doing something I loved! Performing is in my nature and I could lose myself in the performance. No wonder I never put on any weight! I was permanently on the go and I rarely ate. I'd say I was fitter than any GAA player back then, despite the fact that I smoked like a trooper. Everyone smoked back then, everyone.

After my summer in Granard and back in Dublin I took up my 'line' with Lorraine properly and decided I was going to settle down and take responsibility for my own life. I asked Lorraine to marry me and she was thrilled. She told me she not only loved me, she adored me and she knew we were going to be totally happy together. Maybe we could have been. We bought an engagement ring, a relatively cheap one, but madly expensive by standards of the time, and we celebrated by entering a dance competition. I don't think we won but it didn't matter; we were young, beautiful and having fun.

I was still only eighteen and Lorraine seventeen but we were Romeo and Juliet, soul-mates, blah, blah, blah. I was, and still am, a complete romantic and the strong attachment I felt for Lorraine was more like a crush that one girl might have for another in early teenage years. An adulation that is reciprocated. We were ridiculously young for marriage and totally immature of course, but I desperately, desperately wanted my own family; I wanted a little unit of my own. Me, Lorraine and babies. That would make me happy, make me normal, the family man protecting his wife and kids from all the badness in the world. After the dancing competition we held our engagement party in Searson's pub (now the Portobello) on Portobello Bridge and my cousin Mary came to the party with two new-found friends. They were schoolmates of hers from Loreto on the Green. They were divinely beautiful – mixed-race girls with real Afros – their mother was Irish and their dad, Kenyan.

These girls, Andrea and Maria, were so exotic to us. We were starved for a bit of diversity then and when we saw it we loved it and were attracted to those who were different to ourselves. Aunt Sybil was involved in some way with the Jesuit order and she often put up priests who were home from the missions. I got to know one of these priests, Fr Martin, who stayed with her over the years. Fr Martin was very involved in missionary work and lots of men and women of different nationalities would come knocking on Aunt Sybil's door looking for him. Of course I thought all of this was exciting, I loved anything that was even slightly exotic, anything in any way different from the humdrum of a rainy Irish day.

After our engagement party a big gang of us ended up back in Aunty Sybil's house and I can still hear her saying, "My God, Eamon Tallon! You're far too young to be getting engaged!"

"Your aunt is right. You will waste your life if you marry so young," Andrea chipped in – her beautiful exotic face so intent and serious.

I listened to her that night and couldn't stop thinking

of her over the next few days. I was almost obsessed. Andrea was very, very beautiful and so very different to any other girl I knew. I tossed and turned, weighing up all the pros and cons. Lorraine and I only ever made love once. I avoided sex, was terrified my secret would out me. I'm a very sensuous person and I think now, callow youth and all that I was then, that I gave her pleasure. But my own physical pleasure just didn't feel right. It's not that I was ashamed or that it was against my morality code. I couldn't explain it then and perhaps I'm not doing a very good job of explaining it now. I just knew what it wasn't – not what it should be. It just didn't feel like something I ought to be doing with Lorraine.

I loved her and felt more comfortable with her than anyone. With the wisdom of hindsight, I can see that I loved her as women love their female friends, and I understood her love for me in the way a woman understands a friend fancying some fella. I couldn't get to grips with homosexual attraction. I just knew I didn't feel about men what gay men felt about men. That I didn't have that aggressive, stalking instinct that I could see in gay friends. Work that one out! Then try to imagine an undereducated eighteen-year-old in the late 70s trying to work it out!

I did feel that Lorraine wanted me to make love to her, but that feeling wasn't reciprocated by me. I thought about all this – inasmuch as I thought about anything back then – and I decided that the reason I didn't feel particularly physically attracted to Lorraine must be because I was trying to love the wrong woman. I was tremendously attracted to Andrea and thought that she maybe she might be 'The One'. In later years I realised that the only woman I needed to love properly was myself.

I plucked up enough courage within the next week to go to Lorraine and tell her we'd made a mistake, that it wasn't her it was me and I was really sorry but I wasn't ready for the whole marriage business just then. She cried and I cried too but she let me go without too much fuss. Typical Lorraine, sweet, sweet child.

That summer, the summer of 1977, I got my first Afro and I took my first foreign holiday. Jesus, that passport picture was so horrendous! I deliberately lost it a year or two later. It wasn't the only time I 'lost' a passport either. I am incredibly vain and if I grow out of the passport photo I grow out of the passport. My first 'female' passport was the only one I treasured.

I set off for a fortnight in the Canaries with a gang of friends. We partied for a fortnight and it was glorious – all-night dancing, all-day sunbathing and lots of fun – I just loved the nightclubs there. I came back to Dublin after that holiday as the corniest Spanish tourist ever; deep deep tan, looking fantastic with a big Mexican hat with tassels, a big toy donkey, poster with a picture of myself dressed as a Toreador, and a Spanish lady for the window sill of my bedroom. I cringe when I think of it now.

After I broke up with Lorraine, I kept bumping into Andrea, at my aunt's house or at discos and, a month or so after my relationship with Lorraine ended, I started dating Andrea.

I did flit between the two of them over the next six months, when I was with Lorraine I'd think *'This is right'*, then I'd meet Andrea and think *'No, this is the girl I love.'* It's a wonder the two of them didn't kill me for messing them around. But that's me, or rather was me: always attracted to the brightest burning light. A moth fluttering in to be singed. I often think of Lorraine, with great, great fondness – she was part of me, and still has a piece of my heart.

The exotic creature who told me I was too young to marry at nineteen obviously only meant it when it related to someone other than her. We were madly in love but it was an extremely volatile relationship from day one. Andrea liked to get her own way, as did I, and two prima donnas in any relationship were bound to cause tension. We would have the most god-awful rows at nightclubs in front of everyone, usually to do with me talking to other girls and not paying Andrea enough attention, or her dancing with a different man if I was on the podiums dancing. We would end up screeching insults at each other. Then one of us, usually me, would sheepishly approach the other the following day and apologise and everything in the garden would be rosy again.

We were engaged on my twentieth birthday. Why I assumed a wedding was going to change everything is beyond me – my pure romanticism again. Our relationship was just that – a romance. Two people –

one still an emotional child – looking for love and thinking they had found it in each other.

Over my teenage years I did have one or two brief encounters with men. Nothing sexual, just an awareness of attraction. But I worked with gay men in the hairdressing business and I knew from listening to their talk that I quite simply wasn't the same as them. I thought these were my alternatives, either be a gay man and live that life, which quite simply didn't feel right or marry and have the whole family bit. One very dear friend, who was gay, tried to dissuade me from marrying.

"Eamon, have you any idea what you're doing? This is so wrong – you must see that this is wrong."

"I just can't do the whole gay thing," I said. "I'm not gay."

I think he thought I was in denial. I dressed effeminately and my mannerisms would always have been girly. But I wasn't closeted. I just felt gay wasn't right for me – I was attracted to straight men and my instincts were those of a heterosexual woman. But I didn't think I could be a heterosexual woman – this is not something I would have ever come across in my life. I didn't read very much back then and I don't know that there was much information out there about the issue. The advent of the Internet means everyone can share information and there is no reason for anyone to remain ignorant of third-gender issues.

I felt so comfortable, unthreatened, with women and I reckoned I would quite easily be able to live with one.

My thinking, if I thought at all – which I don't think I did – would have been along the superficial lines of: well, Andrea is beautiful and I'm good-looking too, we're both talented and popular and look well together, and we'll have the most divine-looking children. I'm fully aware how superficial that is. But that is the way I thought or rather didn't think. I just ploughed ahead until I got what I thought I wanted, got what I thought would be the thing – 'The One', who would make me a happy, normal human being. I was definitely under-developed emotionally at this stage – classic results I'm told of poor parenting and the sexual abuse I had suffered – in fact, I think I only grew up emotionally in recent years – I was even underdeveloped physically. I tried to grow a moustache in my late teens and shaved it off in disgust after a month when Mum laughed at me and called it "five-a-side".

We put more energy into planning the wedding than we ever did into our relationship. We decided it was going to be a big do, and we were determined to have the best of everything. My mum didn't want us to get married. I'm sure she must have suspected there was something awry but dared not speak its name, and she tried to stop us. But I was twenty-one in June 1979, a legal adult, and on August 18th 1979 I planned to get married. I was going to do the whole thing right: wife, babies, white picket fence, rambling roses, etcetera etcetera.

The night before I got married I was in Zhivago's nightclub and Lorraine came up to me and begged me not to marry Andrea. She cried and cried and I cried too, doubts hounding me and guilt over reducing Lorraine to this state.

But I had just planned the most fashionable wedding Dublin had ever seen. I had to go ahead. I could not have borne to lose face at the time. *It'll be alright* I thought, *everything will work out – just like it's meant to be.* I chose Andrea's dress, the bridesmaids' dresses, flowers, table decorations – everything. I was going to have the perfect wedding, the perfect marriage, the perfect family. Nothing would deflect me from my big day out. Mum had no control over me. Andrea's mum liked me and I loved both her and Andrea's granny. I felt so at home with those lovely women. They were very, very welcoming and they thought we were a good match. We certainly looked well together and were both obsessed with image and appearance. It wasn't uncommon for people to marry in their late teens, early twenties back then. Nowadays people tend to wait until they are in their late twenties or early thirties and have a bit of life behind them before they settle for marriage, mortgage and family.

We had a ball on the day of the wedding. Beauty and fun all the way. Andrea looked absolutely amazing. I'd chosen all the clothes and we thought we were a beautiful fashionable couple and, worse, we thought that being a beautiful fashionable couple was what mattered. Appearance is still important to me, but it's not the be-all and end-all of everything as it can be when you're younger. Andrea wore a white, almost

Grecian style dress that skimmed her boobs. It was practically backless and fell in layers of chiffon to the ground with a side slit – she was incredibly elegant in a time of huge wedding dresses and big hair – stunning, exotic and different.

Of course I can now admit that I wanted every stitch she wore for myself! I so envied her that dress – but I clamped down the thought immediately. I still remembered the fear I'd felt when our neighbour had caught me trying on Lucy's Communion dress fourteen years earlier. I just loved Andrea's wedding dress – I thought it was so sensuous and beautiful. My only fear though was that Auntie Maureen would have a fit – "Oh my God, what is she wearing into the church?!"

But Andrea could get away with it because she was so small-breasted, and I picked up a lovely little ostrich-feathered shrug to go over the dress and white satin sandals with three diamante straps. Her hair was up and in gentle, soft little curls around her face – like the girl in the Cadbury's Flake ad at the time, a white feather in her hair. Divine, divine, divine.

I stayed in Aunty Sybil's the night before the wedding and I do know I was feeling extraordinarily calm the next morning. I can still hear Aunty Sybil laughing and shaking her head as she watched me eating a boiled egg for my breakfast.

"Will you look at the aise of that fella? Not a care in the world!"

I laughed. It was true. I didn't have a care in the world. I just wanted to enjoy the most fashionable

wedding Dublin had ever seen. The only thing bugging
me was the fact that, to go with my oatmeal suit and
skinny tan tie, I had a pair of tan loafers. I hated those
shoes because they were flat. I had wanted the height a
pair of platforms or a wedge heel gave me but I couldn't
get the right colour so had to do with flatties. They
irritated me all day!

The bridesmaids were beautiful as well, one was
Andrea's sister and the other her friend. I dressed them
in white blouses and flared skirts dashed with purple
and they sported little pillbox hats with net. This was
1979! I was so ahead of my time; people were talking
about it as the fashion wedding of the year!

I defy any other Irish husband out there to describe
his bride's outfit like that without the benefit of
photographs thirty years later! 'Ah she wore an aul'
dress, I think it was white.' Lads! Then ye wonder why
ye drive the wives mad!

The wedding reception was in the Clarence Hotel on
Dublin's quays and we danced the night away.
Hundreds of people attended, friends and family on
both sides. After the wedding we went to honeymoon in
London and stayed with Andrea's relatives. London was
kicking off at the time, August 1979, and it was heaven
for the pair of us. Lots of boutiques, bigger shops,
exclusive little clubs and bars. Teeming with people. We
couldn't believe the throngs of people – particularly of
young people. Up to this I had thought of myself as
sophisticated and urbane but London made me feel like
an alien – but an alien who was glad he had landed in

this particular part of the world! Aunty Maureen and Uncle Pat had given us £500 as a wedding present. This was a huge sum at a time when most people of our ages – with good jobs – were earning about £45-£50 a week.

The flat Andrea and I stayed in was near Kings Cross and we had a blast: out all afternoon, evenings and night, and we only ever went back to her aunt's place if we needed a wash and a change of clothes. We walked around Oxford St and the city centre and saw sights we had never even dreamed of. During the day, not only at weekends like at home, you could find musicians or artists down about the centre and some of the most wonderful and bizarre clothes shops we had ever seen. Different, totally different to the Dublin scene.

We blew every penny of Aunt Maureen's money on clothes – beautiful trendy clothes and shoes. Andrea was as mad about clothes as me. It was a shared passion and we could shop for hours without becoming bored. The variety of everything in London was so much greater to what we had at home in Dublin – we were young, beautiful and the way we looked was the only thing that mattered.

Clothes were my first real addiction. I definitely have an addictive personality – whether such a thing exists or not, I definitely have it. I would have gone hungry to buy an article of clothing I wanted. In fact I know I spent many nights walking home from town to Rathmines or Ranelagh. I'd have the money for a taxi, but if I didn't get a taxi, then I could afford some top, or pair of shoes or 'slacks' (Jesus, I hate that word!) that

I had to, had to, had to have. On pissin' rain nights, freezing, miserable nights, I often traipsed home with no coat or umbrella and probably in shoes that were totally unsuitable for walking in! I must've been mad – but you know I think to this day if I saw something, a top or a pair of shoes that I really, really wanted, I would probably do exactly the same thing. Once an addict etcetera!

I can still see Andrea trying on a pair of red boots in a London boutique. They had an almost Cuban heel on them, which was really unusual then, and the leg of the boot stretched up and over the knee. She looked divine in them. I wanted the bloody things for myself and felt guilty about the envy. Andrea baulked a little at the price.

"Get them, get them," I said. "They were made for you. You have to have them!"

I felt so proud of her and when we came home I loved strolling hand in hand across Portobello Bridge dressed to the nines and Andrea in those thigh-high, bright red boots. It was in-your-face fashion. Her lovely skinny jeans tucked into these glorious boots. She was beautiful. I'm trying to bring back more of the honeymoon – but it's such a lifetime ago and I have blocked so much of that time of my life out for so long that it is difficult to recall feelings with much accuracy. I don't remember it as being a special, whistles-and-bells time or a particularly unhappy time – it just 'was'.

I did love her and I think she loved me, we certainly both said we did and, yes, it was love of a sort. I thought her divine and exotic, and I think she may have felt the same about me. I too was someone completely different to other young men of my age – I paid her more attention and danced to her every whim. We were both Geminis and I think there were four people getting married at our wedding. We obviously slept together and had sex and we both enjoyed it. I loved touching Andrea's skin: it was so soft and smooth. But the sex wasn't frequent and we were (or I was at least) just as comfortable kissing and cuddling for a while and then spooning in behind her to sleep. I thought I would be able to pull it off, that now I was married I would be 'fixed' and would have no more thoughts of being different. I had found 'The One'. But we were very, very young and that fact and the fact that we both had dramatic temperaments probably should have signalled the inevitability of where we would end up. It was a dangerous relationship, the first of many.

I think we stayed for a week or maybe ten days in London on our honeymoon. We argued a lot and made up by buying clothes together – lovely London clothes.

When we came back to Ireland I got a job first with Gilbeys Wine Merchants, then switched to the Speakeasy, a bar in Dublin. After a few months at that I got a better job with L'Oreal as a colour technician. I didn't particularly like that job but the money was okay, my name was well known through the industry and I got plenty of work. I was still messing around in bitty jobs at night: a bit of PR, dancing, or bar-work in nightclubs, anything to bring in a few pounds – both

Andrea and myself were high-maintenance. My dream was to own my own salon some day. I knew everyone couldn't be wrong and everyone said I was a gifted hairdresser. And yet. And yet. I never believed it. There was this tiny hard nut at the core of me, this wizened, little cancer. *'You're no good. You're a loser. Nobody really loves you. It's all a fluke and you're going to be found out.'* So to shut that voice up, I had to be the brightest, loudest, most flamboyant and of course the most attractive person going, and I had to have all the best-looking, most popular people around me.

I know now that a lot of this behaviour is common in addicts, alcoholics and people with dependencies that are bad for them. For some reason we just don't love ourselves. But back then I just tried to make my internal monologue as prosaic as I could. I would only think at a very superficial level, about the physical things I had to do on a daily basis; what I wore, where I worked or who I was with. I avoided any in-depth analysis of my thoughts, I barely even acknowledged to myself that I had issues that needed to be dealt with. Some days I would curse God or Mother Nature for making me feel in a way that society told me wasn't normal, didn't exist and was sinful. I knew I was attracted to men in the same way women were because I could fully empathise with these women when they talked about how they felt. Although I was to all outward appearances a part of male society, I had not the slightest notion what went on inside a man's head. I still don't! But I knew at my inner core, my deepest most hidden level, that the lie I was living had to be wrong, and was doomed to failure from the outset. I did not acknowledge this to myself then. It is only now and with the benefit of hindsight and a life lived that I can see how many mistakes I made, how many people I hurt. I never set out to hurt anyone. I knew that I loved Andrea as I had loved Lorraine – but, again with hindsight, I loved them as friends. I wasn't possessive with people then. I was needy certainly, and given my upbringing and early sexualisation that is no surprise, and I accepted all crumbs of affection thrown my way; but, for the rest of it, any niggling concerns I entertained about my marriage, my wife and our sex life were drowned out with work, music, dance, shopping and more shopping. Busy, busy, busy, busy!

In August 1979, Dublin was in a turmoil getting ready for the Papal visit. I was so excited. The Pope. The Father of my Church, coming to say Mass in my city. I remember that morning in late September 1979. We were married a little over a month and had been out dancing late the night before. We had a little flat in Grove Park in Rathmines and I was up, showered, dressed, rosary beads in pocket by 8 a.m., ready to go to the Phoenix Park where John Paul II was due to say Mass. This was totally alien behaviour for night-owl me, but I was probably as excited about the Pope coming as I had been about my wedding. But I could not persuade, inveigle or threaten Andrea from the bed. I was furious. What had I done? Here was this really holy Pope, the loveliest Pope our Church had ever seen – a kind and gentle, charismatic man – coming to say a few special open-air Masses for the first time in Ireland, coming to bless us all and to spread love and goodwill, and my heathen of a wife wouldn't bestir herself from under the bedclothes!

Off I went on my own to see the Pope. Apart from the million other people, that is. I did a lot of thinking that day and made some decisions about my life as I listened to the Mass in the company of all the other hundreds of thousands of smiling Irish people. My heart filled with love for everything God had given me and I was determined to put my best foot forward. More than anything I wanted a family of my own, a cosy little unit where I could feel safe.

I have the wife, I thought, *now all I need is the proper setting, then everything will be normal, I'll stop feeling unsure, and Andrea and I will stop fighting if I'm earning enough money to keep us both happy.*

The place I had felt most secure all my life and the place I wanted to start that proper family life in was obvious to me. I had to start again in Granard.

But I had to wait for the right moment.

7

Daddy Long Legs

I moved from colour technician to sales with L'Oreal, selling their products all over the country and I was good at it – well, at the selling bit, the chatting to people and the whole believing in the product bit. But. But. It was *boring!* And all the stupid administration and accounts! This sort of stuff is not my strong point; it frustrates me and I end up getting myself into the most awful mess. The salary and commission this job brought was good and I had a company car as well. I was good at sales and most salons in Dublin knew me well – in general we all got along and they would tend to buy from me. Then I started to travel down the country a bit, going to salons in big provincial towns, making new contacts and meeting lots of new people. Andrea was lonely when I was away and didn't like staying on her own in the flat so she would go up to her mum's and stay.

My salary didn't rest in the collective marriage purse for long – we both liked to spend. I'm quite sure we horrified our more conservative and thrifty elder relatives but we were young. No longer free or single, but . . . one must always forgive youth!

The fighting between us eased off a little. We were both away from each other for most of the day and sometimes I could be away for three or four days a week travelling around the country. Sometimes she would fall asleep before me and I would lie looking at her, fighting the thoughts popping into my head. Did I love her? Surely everyone had these doubts? Everyone said the first few years were hard. Maybe I did love her enough but what if that love was hiding something else?

Maybe I wanted to be her?

This was a huge thought and I don't know that it was as coherent as that then. It is now, a lifetime later, but I'd say if I'd acknowledged thoughts like those then I would have choked with fright. Bury it, bury it, bury it. It was too much to handle. I had to make this marriage work. Whatever my feelings were, they had no name that I knew of, and I feared I would be rejected by everyone if I admitted them. I refused to be depressed about it. I was young, fit, healthy, making a good living and married to an attractive woman. I could conquer the world if I put my mind to it. Sorted, right?

One night in late spring 1980 when I arrived home from work, Andrea told me she was pregnant. I was ecstatic. A baby! My baby! Made from me and Andrea! This was it – the family I always wanted. I was so overjoyed I ran across to Aunty Sybil's house straightaway and herself and Jack laughed at how delighted I was.

I couldn't wait, and I started planning my child's life straight away. I was the original headless-chicken husband – running about for the first few days helping her. I'm sure I drove Andrea mad. I excused all her little moods for the next while on the grounds of 'hormones'.

We moved to Templeogue and rented a house. Andrea was then working in Gilbeys and I had moved back from L'Oreal to the Speakeasy, where most of my work was night work. I would get home at three in the morning, potter about for a few hours then slip into bed beside Andrea about six. She'd get up at seven to go to work. When she came home I would be heading back out again to my job. We rarely saw each other, but I felt so grown-up. I was living in a house with my wife and I was going to be someone's Daddy! I was actually a caricature of an expectant first-time dad when I think of it now – but that's how big a thrill it was to me. Male friends – hetero male friends – admit to a certain hunter/gatherer type pride and protective feelings towards their 'women' when they are 'with child'; but when I look back at Andrea's pregnancy I can see now that my initial reaction was more that of an overawed younger sister. Delighted, delighted, delighted at the news!

But I did feel enormously proud to have played such a huge role in this new life growing in Andrea and our marriage levelled out into a relative contentment. Maybe the baby would be the making of us.

Above all though, I knew I had a duty – a moral and

physical responsibility to provide for my wife and coming child, and I was determined to set up a safe little family unit, build up a good business and have a loving home into which we could bring our child. I decided now was the time to fulfil the decision I had made at 'the Pope's Mass' in the Phoenix Park. We would move lock, stock and barrel to Granard. I prayed to our Lady and asked for guidance. I felt it was the right thing to do for my little family.

I got really excited about this project and quit my job. Andrea wasn't mad about the idea at first – she had come down to Granard with me on one or two occasions and, although she loved the countryside and the peace, she knew she would miss her family and the shops and clubs of city life. But she knew I was trying to do my best for us all and that in Granard I would have both financial and emotional support from my extended family so she agreed to give it a go.

People knew me in Granard and on visits down over previous years I had started to do the odd cut, colour and blow-dry in women's homes. Women liked what I did to their hair and I would even occasionally get a phone call in Dublin asking me to go down to do hair for someone who was getting married. I thought it would be a good place for a salon. There was no competition in the town then and people had to travel to Longford or other nearby bigger towns to get their hair styled. We had very little money and all our worldly possessions fitted into four bin bags. But we didn't care – we were young and invincible.

What on earth made me, made either of us, think that Andrea – a young city girl – was ever going to be happy in the claustrophobic atmosphere of a small rural Irish town? No matter how much we said we loved each other that strain was bound to bring the walls of our marriage crashing down.

I genuinely believed at the time that if we lived in Granard all our arguing, all the tension and irritability would go away. For wouldn't I be at home and everyone would love Andrea and everything would be fine? Poor Andrea, the poor *cratúir* – for this I am truly sorry. I should never have expected her to adapt to small-town life. If Andrea had had her support structure about her we might have stood a better chance, although our marriage could never have lasted – there was one woman too many in it. We bickered a lot – about everything but not about the mistake we had made in getting married. With the benefit of hindsight I can now identify the rows as the dramatic sort of fights teenage girls have with their friends. But those first few years might not have been so unhappy if we had stayed in Dublin.

So in early summer 1980 I approached the bank where my family had done business for years and arranged a business loan to cover the cost of establishing a salon in one of the houses on Main Street, Granard. We rented a house to live in, opposite Aunty Maureen's house, and near all my old friends and relatives. I knew everyone in the town. Andrea knew no-one and she hated the way people looked at her. She thought they were being nosey but she was just so different to them; she fascinated them – aren't we all attracted to something that's different to the usual? The locals wondered how on earth a young plug of a lad from Granard had managed to snare himself this exotic girl.

I arranged to have my salon in one of the buildings at the other end of the street from the house we were renting, and thanks to the bank loan and some support from Aunty Maureen, I put the best of equipment and products into it. I called it Scruples and was determined it would succeed. I wanted to earn enough money so that in the long term we could buy a house in Granard. This salon would be the making of us. Money coming in would help settle her, I thought. I worked my butt off. I was gone from half seven in the morning and often wasn't home until ten at night. Granard is set in the middle of an agricultural community and the pace of life is usually dictated by cattle or crops and always, always by weather. So I could be doing a cut 'n' blow-dry or a set at either 7 a.m. or 8 p.m. It didn't matter: whenever the client wanted it was when the client got it.

I would drop home at lunch-time to check all was okay and Andrea would just be getting up. Sometimes she might wander down to the salon. But she had absolutely nothing in common with any of my clients and nothing to keep her occupied except the television while I worked.

The inhabitants of Granard and its hinterlands all knew me, knew my people and our history as I knew them and theirs. Andrea was like an exotic bird grounded temporarily amongst a flock of quite happy squabbling starlings. So she started to spend more and more time in Dublin with her mum and family as the pregnancy progressed. I can honestly say I don't think she ever spent a full week in the house in Granard during that pregnancy. I don't blame her – she was young, scared and bored. I was gone twelve to fourteen hours a day trying to earn as much cash as possible to cover house rent, salon rent, bank-loan repayments and simple things like food, electricity bills, heating bills etcetera etcetera. When I'd come home she might be in a bad mood and she'd had the whole day to worry some little irritant into a big grievance. I would be exhausted and in my tiredness I would snap back at her and the row would escalate into another reason for her to go back to Dublin. I used to think she would deliberately try to rile me so she could have an excuse to catch the bus and get away. In fact, I often drove her up in the evening after work, turned around and drove back to Granard, then I would drive up again later in the week to collect her. Andrea didn't drive at the time.

As for the hairdressing itself, it was mostly 'sets' back then – even in the early 80s. Anyone who could afford to go to the hairdresser's regularly were generally 'well set' years-wise which meant rollers, more and more bloody rollers! I loved all my customers and always enjoyed them but my creativity was dying to explode out of me, and my heart would leap when some adventurous young one would come in and say; "Do whatever you want, just make me look different." It didn't happen too often. Life in any small community can be stifling and it can be hard to be original, everyone watching everyone else – not maliciously – but close scrutiny can stifle creativity and imagination in some and make them afraid to look any different from their peers. At least that's the way it was back then. Maybe it's different now. I hope so.

We had decided that our baby would be born in Dublin, although I would have loved it if he or she could have been born in the nursing home in Edgesworthtown where I had been born. But Dublin made more sense, particularly towards the end of the pregnancy. I was working all hours and Andrea's mum and sisters were in Dublin to help her out. The baby was due the first week of December and there were a few false alarms. On December 22nd I got a phone call to say Andrea had gone into the hospital but they didn't think the birth would be quick. My hands were full – any hairdresser will tell you how manic every day is in Christmas week. I think I had every farmer's wife within a twenty-mile radius of the town in that day from 7 a.m. to 5p.m., when I was due to close anyway. I locked up and rushed back to the house for clothes and other bits and bobs, and I got in the car and hit the road.

I was about thirty miles into the trip when I realised I had forgotten something – I can't remember now what that was – Christmas presents perhaps. So I turned around and headed back, and as I got near the town I could see a lot of smoke and I wondered had someone's chimney caught fire. But it wasn't a chimney – it was my bloody salon. I don't know what caused it, a fag-end in the wrong place or maybe an electrical fault. Aunty Maureen and Uncle Pat and half the town were out watching – worrying it would spread along the terrace to businesses and homes.

All my products! Bloody expensive conditioners, colours and all sorts of chemicals, and then all my electrical stuff, hairdryers, sterilisers – everything. I tried to get in to save stuff but Maureen grabbed a hold of me.

"Eamon, Eamon – you can't go in – you'll be killed! Sure it's only aul' shampoo and stuff. Look at the hold the flames have on the place – here's the fire brigade. Let them try!"

Granard has a reserve fire-fighting unit and as Maureen spoke the fire brigade did arrive and soon had the blaze under control. The salon was destroyed and it was a miracle that it was the only building damaged when you think of the amount of highly flammable chemicals that are stored in a salon. The Gardaí were there too and it was really late before I drove away that night. Remember, there were no mobile phones then. Those who were waiting for me in Dublin assumed I was on the road so they didn't phone Granard to see where I was and I didn't phone Andrea's mum because I didn't want Andrea worrying.

I drove straight to the Coombe Hospital and although visiting was over they let me in. It was the most incredible moment of my life, that first sight of my baby daughter. I can still smell my darling girl, feel those tiny fingers gripping mine, see her tiny jaundiced little face – she looked like a tanned porcelain doll – perfect. I had never ever seen anyone as beautiful. It was instant love. I don't think I slept that night. I stayed with Mum in the apartment in Dartry, where she was living at the time, and I sat up half the night on her sofa, thinking, all excited. I finally dozed off and was back at the hospital at the earliest possible minute.

I cannot describe holding my precious daughter in my arms. There are simply not enough words in my vocabulary. Anyone who has parented a child knows the feeling. Complete awe, devotion and an immediate incredibly protective and unconditional love. It is still the same feeling I get whenever I think of her. My Ava, my child.

Andrea's labour had been tough and she was exhausted. I think I was more upset about missing the birth than she was about it. It was only in the 70s that fathers had finally been admitted into labour wards. Up to that, it was midwifes and doctors only and it was still something of a novelty to have dad in the delivery suite – but I had so wanted to be there.

Andrea was shell-shocked. She'd had a really hard time and she had thought she was going to die. I felt so sorry for her. I held both of my girls and swore everything would be all right now. I stayed with them for as long as the hospital let me and we talked when she felt up to it. I gave Ava her little bottles, changed her nappies and held her. When I walked away from the hospital later that day I thought my heart would burst with pride. I wanted to shout it from the rooftops, tell everyone – I was a parent! Me! I had my own little family unit – at last.

People question why I got married, why I lived later as a gay man etcetera etcetera, how I hurt Andrea by allowing us to be married in the first place. I understand the questions and everyone should be aware that none of my actions were ever intended to hurt anyone. In reading or hearing other accounts of transgender people of my generation the reader will discover that it is not uncommon for transgender people to marry the wrong sexual partner, considering the confusion they feel is the normal 'pre-wedding' jitters others talk of. Many of us may parent children before realising that we cannot continue to live the lie we have been living. It does not make us horrendously selfish or self-deluded people. Simply human and fallible. Being different is not easy; everyone wants to conform to the 'norm', to fit in to the society around them, be happy and go with the flow, particularly in the first thirty years of life. I did not choose my gender, no more than any one of you reading this. My genomes or DNA or whatever made that decision.

I do regret marrying Andrea, for she was the next victim of Nature's mistake and of both my ignorance and Irish society's ignorance of my gender dysphoria. I was the first victim. But I can't regret the marriage for producing my daughter. Ava is the most positive part of my life.

In 1979, I could not have expressed how ambivalent

I was about my sexuality, let alone my gender. I didn't know what my choices were. I didn't have the words. I was what I was. I am what I am. I loved Andrea, but at twenty-one (an emotionally stunted and immature twenty-one) and with precious little education, how could I have seen what lay ahead? Life is a journey and I took a few wrong turnings. As do we all.

I can now see that my love for Andrea, and for Lorraine before her, was the type of love that we women bear for our female friends. I mistook that empathy for the type of love that leads people into marriage. An empathy with another human being, someone who was interested in me, in what I thought, in my life. Someone to love, just for me.

When I look at my marriage, and also later relationships, I can see how the sexual abuse I was subject to as a young child damaged me. It made me desperate for love, attention, respect. All the things my abusers had not given me. They selected me and used their power over me to physically hurt me and mentally scar me. Forever. You do not walk away lightly from any type of abuse. It ruins lives, wrecks people. Those of us that have come through know that. All we can do is tell everyone else about it. We all must make sure it is never, ever allowed to happen again. Society is now aware of what is at stake. Our children's choices and chances of happiness in life must not be stolen from them by indecent people.

We took baby Ava back to Granard and I re-established the salon in another shop unit on the Main

Street. I was every inch the proud parent. I loved pushing Ava in her buggy. *Look at me! I'm a parent!* I loved people coming up to ooh and aah over my tiny princess and some of the older women saying, "Eamon! Isn't it great to see fathers out pushing the prams? Life surely is changing!" You have to remember Ireland was about twenty (or a hundred and twenty) years behind the rest of the Western World in attitudes to things like parenting, sexuality, morality – most things really. And who kept us there?

Andrea started spending a lot of time in Dublin again. Her grandfather died and they were a close family and gathered together to comfort each other. We drifted along in our marriage. There was no sexual attraction between us, we very rarely made love. It didn't bother me – but it did set Andrea thinking. We tried. We really tried. I would help with Ava as much as I could. When she got a little older I would take her down to the salon in the morning with me so that Andrea could rest and have some 'me' time. I didn't want 'me time', for 'me time' meant thinking. Thinking was to be avoided at all costs. Like Scarlett O'Hara I would always *think about it tomorrow*.

By 1982 and the time Ava was fifteen months old, Andrea and she were practically living in Dublin while I ran the business in Granard. I had to do something. It was impractical for everyone involved. But it was Andrea who took the bit between her teeth. She was the courageous one. We were walking down the South Circular Road one day and I was pushing the buggy.

Andrea had been quiet all day and I asked her was something wrong.

"Do you think you're gay?" she asked.

I was aghast – it had been said, a possibility posed that I had already thought about but buried because I knew at my deepest level that 'gay' was not what I was. I can still feel my shock and burning embarrassment and see her face, the bewilderment in both of us.

I do not have an aggressive nature but that day I pushed her. She actually stumbled a few steps back onto the road. Andrea's question and my reaction to that question was the final blow our marriage needed. I didn't answer her, my reaction and the look on my face told her she had hit on a truth.

There was actually no further discussion on the subject. We were staying with relatives of Andrea's in Walkinstown and when we got back to that house I packed a bag and left. It was as simple, unplanned and inevitable as that.

I was reluctant to leave, particularly to leave Ava, but with hindsight I also remember a small sigh of relief. It had been said, I was 'outed'. I was terribly embarrassed. A bit ashamed too, although I knew it wasn't something I had chosen to be. Whatever I saw in the mirror no-one else saw. I'd look in the mirror and I'd see a woman. But I wasn't a woman, not according to the manual of life. I did know I was sexually attracted to men and although I didn't want to lose Ava, I knew I couldn't stay married to Andrea and be sane. I also knew, from experience, that a baby needs its mum more than anyone. But I wasn't going to give up without a battle, so I closed the salon in Granard and followed them to Dublin. At least there I might be able to play some role in Ava's life – or so I thought.

8

Banana Republic, Septic Isle . . .

So – my marriage was over. I couldn't say I was sorry or depressed about it for it never really existed. In the three years we were 'together' I'd say we might have only spent one full year of being in the same house at the same time. I don't think anyone in either family was surprised. My own family just wrote it off as 'typical Eamon behaviour'. It must have been tough on Andrea, twenty-three years of age, a broken marriage behind her and a daughter to care for. There was no divorce legislation in Ireland at that time so effectively we were stuck with each other unless Andrea could get an annulment. She did set that process in motion and the marriage was dissolved some years later. I deeply regret having put her through all that. But I couldn't regret Ava; she was the best thing to ever happen to me. I took the ear-bashing from Mum and my family – "typical Eamon – can't stick to anything for long", and tried my best to see as much of Ava as Andrea permitted.

Then, through the contacts I'd made when I worked for L'Oreal, I was 'discovered' by David Marshall of David Marshall Hair and Beauty. David had the first exclusive-type hair salon in Dublin, in Ireland in fact. He set about retraining me which drove me mad at first because having won Young Hairdresser of the Year years ago, and having owned my own salon, I thought my ten years' experience should have excluded me from this. But there was a pecking order in David's salon (quite correctly) and I fitted in as a junior finisher initially, but I knew this was a step up the ladder for me, a good career move that I wanted. I was moved on to stylist fairly quickly, once David saw my willingness to accept his system.

My reputation was growing and the models who came in from Nan Morgan's, Geraldine Brand's and Grace O'Shaughnessey's model agencies – all the top agencies in the country at the time – all looked for me to style their hair. I was always well paid.

I tried my best to provide for my daughter and saw her on Saturdays initially. But my relationship with Andrea became more and more fraught.

At this point there was a big change in my life. Marriage having failed me or my having failed it, I started going to gay bars and clubs and having brief encounters with men. I was out on the town every night – mainly so I didn't have to sit with my own company. I was living the life of a single person, I accepted that I was attracted to men therefore I must be gay, but it still didn't feel right. I didn't quite fit. I knew I didn't think like other gay men did about their partners, nor did I feel as promiscuous or seem to have the same sexual appetite of some of my gay friends. Later I would come to realise that I am monogamous by nature. I have no interest in sex for sex's sake. I need the whole deal, the emotional attachment as well as the physical. The gay scene in Ireland – even in Dublin – at that time was very, very small and kept itself hidden. Gay people didn't legally exist in Ireland nor did people who wanted abortions or divorce nor anyone who challenged the norm in any way.

Andrea got wind of the life-style I was living and she decided that I couldn't see Ava, or play any role in the child's life. In hindsight, of course, I am grateful to her for that. I wasn't mature enough to take care of a child and now I am glad that my daughter wasn't pulled into the chaos that became my life. But at the time I was distraught. I begged and pleaded both in letters and in person. I even cried outside her hall door one night, ringing the doorbell and getting no answer. But to no avail. Whatever rights fathers have now, they had even less in the 80s. I was afraid of going through the courts to get access. I did investigate it but the advice was 'forget about it'. A self-confessed gay person who had married and fathered a child wouldn't have had a leg to stand on in the 'living on the moon' attitude of Irish law, Church and State in 1980s Ireland. Banana Republic.

By early 1983 Ava had been withdrawn completely from my life and, although my career was forging ahead with David Marshall's, I was desperately unhappy without my daughter. I lost myself in work and partying. I was constantly being requested through David Marshall's to go out to fashion shoots and different PR events, preparing models' hair before they were photographed or went on stage to model. I really enjoyed this work. I was meeting these beautiful women, seeing their make-up, the fabulous *haute couture* clothes. My professional reputation was growing and I was the requested stylist by a lot of photographers and magazines – the biggest magazine sellers in Ireland at the time like *U, Irish Tatler* and *Woman's Way* all wanted me. I loved working with other creative people, photographers, make-up artists etcetera – I think this was when I started to use the name Ross Tallon all the time. In 1977, there was a second Eamon working with me in a salon in the Crumlin Shopping Centre and to avoid confusion the manager had asked me could I pick a 'professional' name. It was actually Mum who suggested the name Ross, I have no idea why, but I liked it and so 'Ross' I became – only in work initially but then it stuck and, by the time I worked in David Marshall's, I had started to use it all the time.

My career was going well but, if I couldn't see Ava, my life in Ireland was not worth living and I decided to leave and try my hand in London. Goodbye, Dublin. I left David Marshall's and I remember writing my name in wet cement on Dawson Street just up the street from the salon, leaving my mark on Dublin – that was all that was left of me. I went to The Pink Elephant, a popular club for fashion and media types, with Jason, one of the other stylists in David Marshall's, and we had a few drinks. I was disillusioned and jobless again. I cared about not seeing my daughter but that was all. I thought, *Fuck you, all of you!* I was determined to put as much distance between me and Dublin as I could.

I definitely went into an almost surreal state of mind at this stage and remained in that headspace for a long time, almost floating above myself looking at the mess I'd made, but not part of it. I couldn't be part of it. It would have killed me to see Andrea pushing Ava in her buggy along Grafton Street. Dublin is such a small city you will eventually bump into everyone you ever knew in your life. London was big enough to let me be lost in it.

I was sharing a bedsit with a girl from Northern Ireland in London and this was the time when the seedier side of my life started. In a club in Soho one night we were both moaning about being broke and how hard it was to get reasonably paid work. We were trying all the salons and, although I had built up a reputation for myself in Ireland, London didn't give a damn. It meant nothing there. Someone in the crowd we were with suggested we should give escort work (male to male in my case) a go. At first we were horrified but when we looked into it more, talked to people who had done it and contacted the agency etcetera, we discovered it really was easy money. It was completely respectable. These lonely rich people paid you to be eye candy on their arm! All I had to do was turn up, look good and be pleasant. For that I got £100 an hour. I'd have to clip a lot of heads of hair to make that sort of cash. I'd say that's where my addiction to cash started. I earned big and I spent big.

In hindsight I can see what Ross was doing. He/I was trying anything to drown out my inner voice calling to let my true identity – whatever that might be – emerge. I couldn't think if I was constantly on the go – talking, shopping, working, dancing. But I still had to crawl into bed at night and be with myself and then my mind would start to tick over. On the gay scene in London I was seeing all sorts of combinations and saw many drag queens and transvestites. I met women who had been born in male bodies and had started the road to their correct gender identity and who looked fantastic. It was too much for me to take in. It was like I'd walked into a room and suddenly everyone was talking a language I understood. But it swamped me. I wasn't ready for Rebecca yet and I exhausted myself, making sure I was fit only for sleep as soon as my head hit the pillow.

Between 1983 and 1985 I hopped back and forward between London and Dublin. I had started a relationship, the only long-term, stable one I had as a gay man, with a beautiful Irish boy. Oh Sam! We had this fabulous, tempestuous, disastrous relationship. Sam was a wonderful young man. He was nineteen and I was twenty-four when we met in Dublin and we were almost instantaneously madly in love. I was home and was working at different things. I set up Ross Elliot Tallon's in Ballsbridge and I was helping a close friend Evelyn Barry with the PR work in re-launching her career as a model. A beautiful and kind woman, she later moved to Florida.

Sam was a student and I thought him so intelligent as well as beautiful and funny. But we were poison for each other. Friends spent half their time trying to keep us together or pulling us apart. Not physical violence – just words and dramas; we were both highly-strung, prima donnas. I was with Sam on-and-off for about a year and a half, maybe over almost three years if one added in all the periods we spent apart. When we had a row – which was often – I would flee the country. Dublin was too small to contain both of us and he had to finish his degree. I'd go to London or other European cities, staying with friends or in cheap hotels and we would cruise Soho or its equivalent in Dusseldorf or Amsterdam.

I saw all the possibilities – drag-queens, straight gays, transvestites, transsexuals, transgender, every city seemed to have them all. My mind started to whirr at some of it. Where the hell did I fit? This uncertainty fed through into my relationship with Sam and at one stage, in early 1984, I moved to the Canaries and tried to forget him completely.

It was an idyllic free kind of life – cheap accommodation, no bills or hassle. My friends and I did publicity on the streets in the evening for clubs and bars, and for one particular restaurant – which we always pushed hard because we were guaranteed a meal if we did well!

I cut hair on the beach during the day and we partied late at night.

The reason I'm sure of the date as 1984 is because someone rang to tell me about the death of Anne Lovett and her baby in the grotto in Granard that January. This poor young teenager had hidden her pregnancy from everyone and had gone to the grotto to give birth. It was a bitterly cold night and both Anne and her baby died there, alone but for each other and the watching statues. I didn't know who I felt sorrier for, the misfortunate dead children and their family or my poor little town and the media scrum that would descend on it. Granard had no idea of the rest of the world, Certainly from my perspective at that time, I felt that Ireland had no idea of the rest of the world, it was still such an inward-looking cleric-ridden society.

In the Canaries I came across what were called *travesties* – it was an umbrella term used to describe anyone who liked to dress differently or appear to be different to the gender assigned to them by society. Everywhere I went outside of Ireland I could see how I wasn't a freak, I wasn't alone. There were hundreds of thousands, possibly millions of people just like me. That gave me such comfort that I started to dare to hope that there might be some chance of becoming what or who I felt I was at my core. Ireland seemed more and more backward and provincial to this country child.

In Dusseldorf one evening, I had a long chat with a transgender woman. This woman was highly intelligent and appeared to be living a 'normal' life as a woman.

She was married to a straight guy and worked in a boutique and seemed wholly content with her body and her lot in life. So I saw that my 'condition', for want of a better word, existed all over Europe and was not exclusive to me or to the 'sisters' – a word used to describe the transsexuals, transgenders and transvestites I'd met in London. This lady told me about transgender people all over the world, about huge communities of 'sisters' in Australia and America and how in India 'sisters' have their own caste called Hjera. They have a special Hindu goddess, Bahuchara Mata, whom they worship. Hjera are treated as very special people, intuitive, gentle and sensual, and are largely regarded as bringing good luck by the wider community. The more I heard and the more I saw, the more convinced I became that this was my path. But I didn't discuss it with anyone close to me; a part of me still held back. What about Ava? What if I did get her back into my life, how would a little girl cope with having a father who was a woman?

Throughout all of this period, Sam and I lived together on-and-off as partners. I did love him deeply. I was hair-styling, freelancing mostly, and, with all the lovely 'ladies who lunched' looking for my talents, I was very well paid. I also did photo-shoots with various photographers and model agencies and had plenty of cash to throw around. Andrea would take no money from me so every penny went on my immediate needs – clothes, hair, shoes, travel, more clothes, did I mention shoes? And . . . oh yes . . . clothes. I didn't do anything sensible like buying a house with it.

Although Sam loved me and we had a great relationship – well, lively anyway – he sensed that there was something within me that was not the male sexual partner he wanted, though he couldn't put his finger on it. It would come up in rows between us. Full-on, teenage, no-holds-barred bitchy fights. For example, one day I was queuing to buy a coffee with Louis Walsh and Gerry Lynch in the newly opened Mary Rose coffee shop in the atrium of the Powerscourt Townhouse Centre. Louis had been a neighbour of Mum's in Dartry and I had met him through her. He started to use me to style the hair of the singers and entertainers he managed. It was a big boost to my career and because I was as music mad as Louis we got on well. Johnny Logan was probably his biggest client in Ireland at that time. It was Easter and I had just bought Sam the biggest Easter egg I could find and it was on the floor beside me as we drank our coffee and chatted.

I lifted my head and spotted Sam talking to his ex-boyfriend at the doorway of one of the other shops. I went ballistic. This boy had been hanging around us on-and-off trying to get Sam back. I saw red! I threw the Easter egg as hard as I could from the door of the coffee shop over to the doorway where the men were standing where it smashed onto Sam's head.

I was screaming like a harridan as I rushed at both of them, "You fucking bastard, you lying, cheating fucking bastard!"

Louis and Gerry had followed me in hot pursuit and they had to pull me off Sam. I was wildly lashing out at him and I think they thought I would kill him or at least scar him for life.

I was wearing a pair of petrol-blue leather trousers and a white blouse and I had a pair of flattish boots on with a Cuban heel (note my priorities!). And as Louis and Gerry stood between us, Sam let rip. He gave me the bitchiest insult that can be swapped between gay men: "Do y'know what? You've got an arse like a woman!"

So I left him and I moped about friends' flats for a few days. I was staying with one friend, let's call him Peter, may God love him for he was good to me and looked after me. I was so hurt and in so much emotional pain that Peter would cry because he felt so bad for me.

A week after the Easter egg incident Peter got word that Sam knew where I was staying and was on the way to try and make up with me. Peter was terrified of a scene. He hadn't come out and didn't want these two obviously gay, obviously hysterical men causing trouble either inside or outside his home. His apartment was on the third floor and he chubb-locked me into the apartment and waited outside to head Sam off in another direction.

But love knows no limits and Sam stood outside the apartment building shouting up to me: "Please, please, Ross, please! I love you! Please let me in! Please talk to me! I'm sorry!"

So I, of course, immediately forgave him and I was hanging over the balcony, like Rapunzel, without the hair, or Juliet and crying as well: "I can't let you in, I can't! Peter's locked me in – he doesn't want trouble in his place. Wait!"

So what did I do? I climbed over the balcony and dropped into the arms of my Romeo. And I didn't even break a nail. Aaaah! I was twenty-five – doesn't it sound more like fourteen-year-old behavior? But that was me – full-on at everything I did – even when I loved the wrong people – particularly when I loved the wrong people.

I must've been mad and I definitely must have nine lives, because I had a relatively easy landing in a flower-bed, and we fell into each other's arms and that was that – until the next row. I think that was probably the first time I was really, really in love. That raw passion. It is so glorious and so incredibly heart-breaking.

Sam was great fun and he loved coming to Granard with me. I'm sure Aunty Maureen knew he was my boyfriend but she never said anything. When we were down one weekend I went over to the convent to cut some of the nuns' hair and Sam came with me. We had great fun with the nuns. I tried on one of their veils to see what kind of a nun I'd make and we all agreed I would have made a very serene and pretty nun. They filled us up with cups of tea and bowls of sherry trifle and let me tell you the Mercy nuns in the convent in Granard didn't spare the sherry when it came to the trifle. I came back up to Aunty Maureen half cut after two bowls of that trifle. Aunty Maureen, Sam and myself laughed for half the evening over that incident.

I wish I could have that type of innocent fun back again.

Sam and I broke up for good eventually. There was just one row too many and, even though I loved him, I knew it still wasn't right. I can see now how in every relationship I became dependent on the other person, co-dependent. I never heard that word until I went into recovery. I was totally dependent all my life on other people for my emotional well-being. In any relationship I thought that other person was the one who had to make me happy. I never realised that I was responsible for my own happiness, that true contentment had to come from within and acceptance of myself, with all my flaws and imperfections, was the only way forward. Instead I depended on others to love me, to give me what I could not give myself. It was mentally a very unhealthy way to live.

I had known, after that first glorious burst of passion, that I didn't feel I was doing the right thing or behaving in the right way with Sam. In my trips abroad I had seen all the possibilities that were out in the world and I needed to explore these options. Dublin felt claustrophobic to me and, again, it being so small meant that I was bound to run into Sam – maybe out with a new partner. I would have been so envious that they had the one thing I wanted – someone to love me. Of course I had to learn to love myself first.

So I returned to London and got a job in a salon in Regent Street. One of the managers there could see my talent (he told me so!) and he attached me to a model agency that used his salon and I started to build a portfolio of clients there. Hair and make-up tended to go together in London and, although I hadn't done much make-up work before, I practised on myself and friends and quickly became proficient at it. Soon I was ready to go at it freelance. There was fierce competition at the top of the hair and make-up artist game but I got really good, wealthy clients who were prepared to pay top-dollar for the best. I gave them the best. But during this time I had no real fixed abode. I lived out of a suitcase which I replenished with designer clothes whenever I'd need to. Sometimes I'd rent a flat on a short lease for a couple of months or I'd crash with a friend or my family if I was back in Dublin. Drifting.

It was about this time that a man called Gabriel came into my life. Keep him in your mind for he pops in and out of my story over the next twenty-odd years. I met him in one of the clubs in Soho and he was to become what you might call 'an unstable fixture' in my life. We didn't have a sexual relationship although we occasionally kissed and cuddled, and at times I would have alluded to him as my boyfriend. He was useful to me in some ways – he seemed to know everybody and he could blag his way into, or out of, anything. He was reticent about his background, and as to what he did to earn a crust, I haven't a clue. He did have a great eye for interior design and knew a lot of people in that world but I don't know that he ever earned a living at it. He was the biggest name-dropper I ever met. But he definitely was a very talented interior designer.

I was determined to be successful in London. I would not become the archetypal Paddy in County Kilburn supping warm beer in Biddy Mulligan's and painting rosy pictures of 'the aul' sod', not able to come home for fear of being shown up as destitute.

I had two lives there. I did escort work if freelancing styling work was thin on the ground.

The money became a total addiction and Gabriel was quite happy to help me spend it. My seedier night life and my more glamorous hair styling and fashionable day life meant I had plenty of cash and rarely did my two lives meet. Gabriel would have been aware of both sides of me – in fact, he would have put me in contact with people looking for escorts. But I was always successful Ross when I went to Dublin and never did anything in the least bit disreputable in Ireland – bar getting drunk and making an eejit of myself. I had plenty of money in my back pocket, not telling anyone where the bulk of it was earned.

In late 1985, I came home for a longer spell. I would constantly get homesick in London and fed up with Gabriel sponging off me and need a fix of Ireland for a while. I was offered a job as school principal at Robert Chambers School of Hairdressing in Grafton Street. I liked this work, working with enthusiastic people who were interested in the same things I was interested in. But the day was too structured for me and ever since boarding school I haven't been able to bear strictures; being told what to do and when to do it. It stifled me and the job only lasted about eight or nine months.

Which was a pity because I loved teaching and the student hairdressers seemed to enjoy my teaching.

But my stint in Robert Chambers sowed in me the seed of an idea about setting up my own model agency. The country was full of beautiful, intelligent, talented women and men, and a plan started to form in my brain. I knew the work would be both diverse and buzzy, I'd be involved in fashion and, if I did the hair and make-up as well, I could make good money, and as it would be my business I could call the shots.

I left Robert Chambers and went back to London again in 1986, back to the doing escort work (male to male) again and freelance hair and make-up. Each time I went back to London over the next few years my life got seedier and seedier – I can see that now but I don't think I was aware of it at the time. I didn't care how I earned the money or where it took me. I had no fear. It's a form of self-abuse really, selling yourself to the highest bidder. Letting people pay you to be their 'friend', for a few hours anyway. Gabriel popped up again – he pops up in all my London stints. Have you seen the film *The Passion of The Christ*? Well, Gabriel in my life is like the devil in that movie, always sticking his nose in when you'd least need him! Although I was very glad that Gabriel did this at a later stage in my life.

As I mentioned before, my astrological symbol is Gemini and at that time I was definitely two people. In Ireland, I was Ross Tallon, hairstylist and a career-orientated person. In London, I was also this Ross but with the added identity of Ross the Escort. I switched seamlessly between the two and nobody at home would have been aware of my life in London, and as nobody in London cared about my life at home I could be who I pleased.

I built a formidable reputation for myself and on the surface was a very successful hair and make-up artist to the glitterati. I started to get more gigs and be better known. I worked with a lot of models, particularly from Models One – the leading London model agency – Davina McCall of *Big Brother* fame would have been with Models One at that time. I would have liaised with Davina a lot at a later date when I brought over models from London to Dublin for Tallon Models. Yasmin Le Bon, Twiggy and Linda Evangelista were also represented by Models One at different times. I think Caroline Cossey, better known as Tula, was one of the higher-profiled transgendered women at the time – I really admired this fabulous woman, her temerity to be herself in a cruel and unforgiving business. Mandy and Nicola Smith were among other clients of mine and I actually did Mandy's and the bridesmaids' hair and make-up the morning of her wedding to Bill Wyman of the Rolling Stones. That was the wedding of the year. I actually was on Irish radio that morning. I talked to Gerry Ryan of Radio 2 and gave him the lowdown on all the glitterati at the wedding; I knew Gerry from our pirate-radio days in the late 70s. It was at that wedding that I first met Boy George – we had a few drinks together that day. The whole affair was completely sumptuous and any celebrity within flying distance of London was there. A great day.

As I easily got lost in the big anonymous gay scene in London, I learned more and more about myself. It was here that I gradually learned more about gender and sexuality and the differences between the two. Gender is the sex which you identified most with and behaved like – in my case women. Sexuality is which sex you are attracted to, in my case men. This was a big eye-opener for me and gave me lots of food for thought. But I still wasn't ready to put Rebecca to the test. It was a step too far for me, a bit mad I thought. I still loved to come to Ireland for visits and I didn't think Ireland would ever accept me if I started to live as the woman I knew I needed to be. I got so homesick at times that I still needed my Dublin or Granard fix. Yet I gradually gravitated towards the idea of living as a woman, to the point where I accepted that I eventually would.

Through the escort work I heard of a strip club where they were looking for male pole-dancers willing to bare all. My male body was very slim and lithe – I never ate much and from all the dancing I had done over the years I was very fit. I suppose Ross's body could have been described as being like that of an Asian boy's. The pole-dancing and stripping were okay. I treated it in the same way I treated the escort work – as a performance. On, dancing for half an hour, then off for half an hour. I understand now that all that behavior – the stripping, escort work etcetera – made me feel in control. This time I was in control of men, not the other way around. It was payback for the men who had abused me. Look but don't touch, and pay me for the pleasure of being permitted to look. I wouldn't have been as articulate as that at the time, but I do remember both jobs made me feel powerful. I was the one in charge. There was a satisfaction in that: being in control and taking their money. Hand on heart, I can swear that I never slept with any man at any stage for money. If there was an emotional attachment then, yes, I would have sexual intercourse, but only if I had feelings for the person. And I made him put his wallet away.

But I did treat my body like a business. I was in 'fuck you' mode and I was determined in most cases to screw as much money out of these sad bastards as I could. I hated my body and was quite happy to use it in a way which others might find demeaning. It was merely a means to an end for me. I started experimenting, dabbling only at this stage, with ecstasy and cocaine, and I would be high as a kite a lot of the time, living on another planet away from all the pain – again that surreal feeling. To be honest, I was high as a kite most of the time without doing drink or drugs – the inner battle with Rebecca screaming to be recognised was ongoing and I was frightened of her because I think I sensed how powerful she was.

I missed Ava constantly through all of these years and on her birthdays and other key days I would send presents. I would think; *'She's six now or eight. I wonder what she's like? Is she still a happy child? Who does she look like? How is she getting on in school?'* But I couldn't afford emotionally to let that dictate my life, for if I did I would have to commit suicide, and I reckoned a dead parent is worse than an estranged parent to any child. Busy, busy, busy, that was the key.

I made a huge effort this time with my career and it really did well. My career, my life, seemed great on the surface. I was a young man about town, building a reputation for myself, losing myself in work. Work has been a great escape for me all my life and I always put my heart and soul into whatever job I was at. I was good, I knew I was good – everybody said it and they couldn't all be wrong. So eventually my confidence, at least in that part of my life, began to grow. I spent every night out in clubs, I still had no real interest in drink – which is peculiar given that I'm Irish and was to all intents and purposes a single man with no commitments again. My marriage had died, or more accurately had been a complete false start and I had tried the life of 'a gay man' – although I hate using that term – but that's all they are – words, another label. I knew at this stage that it was definitely men I was attracted to, but not gay men.

Eamon to Ross was a slow transformation. Ross was just a hairdresser's name which had allowed Eamon to evolve into a gay man over a number of years. My family accepted me as Ross and there was an acknowledgement, unspoken but there, that they had always known I was different. It was easy for me in one sense. I just ran to London and other European cities any time life in the pressure-cooker world of fashion/media/music on a tiny island became too much for me. But it was definitely more difficult for my family. People who knew I had a child would ask me about her and I'd say, half fantasizing and wishing I knew – "Oh, she's fine. She's with her mum in Paris." But I couldn't protect my siblings, Mum or my relatives in Granard in the same way. People can be cruel, often unintentionally I'm sure, but it was my family who had to put up with the whispering hands everywhere they went. "See him/her? He/She is a brother/sister/cousin/nephew/whatever of that gay hairdresser who does well for himself up in Dublin or over in London."

This cannot have been easy on anyone. It certainly wasn't on me.

9

Careless Whispers

During the next decade I was to pop in and out of my family's lives. I did try to stay away – I couldn't behave in a way expected of me (or what I felt was expected of me) so I just stayed away. But every so often I would get incredibly homesick. For Granard, for my family and my Irish friends, and I'd come back – just for a little while, flirt for a while with the whole family concept. I even tried setting up my business again on two separate occasions in Granard. Then as soon as I felt threatened or my family did and the heat came on me, I was off again. Flit, flit, flit.

I missed Ava so much and felt completely helpless when it came to her. I had a daughter who I never saw. Her mother wanted absolutely nothing to do with me and was determined that Ava wouldn't either. I didn't even know if the presents I was sending were getting to her, and I was dependent on relatives and friends for snippets of information about her. My cousin Mary was still in touch with Andrea and was the only member of my family who ever saw Ava. But she told me Andrea did not want me to have anything to do with the child and advised me to steer clear. I did, but it wasn't easy. Perhaps I should have fought harder, but mindsets and society were very different back then and I felt that perhaps I had caused Andrea enough trouble at that stage. If she wanted me to stay away I would stay away, but I felt like a piece of me had been torn off and, as I did with everything else, I buried the whole painful issue – let it fester inside me like a cancer on my soul.

In late 1986 and into 1987 I was back in London living in Maida Vale. I always associate the George Michael song 'Careless Whispers' with that time. I would have known George to chat to because we moved in the same social circles at the time and I always loved his songs. By day I was hair and make-up artist to top models – seen in the best shops, coffee shops, wine bars, restaurants, hotels. The hair and make-up business is a tough game and superficial image is everything. You needed cash to keep the image up and I wasn't the only one who did 'extra shifts' as a stripper or an escort at night. Duality – story of my life.

On days I hadn't any hair/beauty photo-shoots on, or sometimes even on days when I did, I would do a shift in one of the strip clubs. I would do a 6p.m. to 11p.m. shift or an 11p.m. to 6a.m. shift. I would walk out of there after one shift with up to £500 in tips plus wages. Huge, huge money at that time. Let's see, context . . . the average house price in England then (not that I wanted an 'average' house back then!) was about £44,000. So 88 stripping shifts – say about three months' work and I could have bought a house for cash. Cash, for something other people took out thirty-year mortgages for.

I think I may have taken a day off once a fortnight, but I never rested, for to rest would be to think. About Ava. About home. About how fucked up my life, sexuality, gender was. About me. I thought I knew the answer to what I was or who I was already – but was too scared to follow my natural path. Some people describe their bodies as temples – mine was a fucking volcano, all this lava gurgling away inside me – just waiting for the chance to blow, raise the roof, knock the top off the pressure cooker and any other metaphor you can find to describe a woman in a man's body screaming: "*LET ME OUT!*"

But what did Ross do? He ran around like a headless chicken working at everything and anything – everything – except confront the real problem.

But within the next two years Ross would be Rebecca and he would have disappeared. Ross was only ever a fabrication, the gay hairdresser who brought me from the child Eamon to the woman Rebecca.

I had already taken a huge step forward in 1988 and begun to use black-market sex-hormone drugs. The treatment for gender dysphoria, both hormonal and surgery, is very pricey. Other trannies or 'sisters' all advised me to start taking black-market hormones to suppress my male hormonal drive and to enhance my female one. I needed cash for these. One of the 'sisters' introduced me to a dealer and he got the medication for me. I was terrified taking them initially. I've always had a difficulty taking pills – I seem to gag on them. Now I was taking handfuls of pills every day. I took two 'female' ones called Prefera and Premerine which softened my skin, gave my face a rounder softer look and encouraged tiny little breasts to grow. My body hair was already minimal and this softened. I was finally on the road to the body I should have been born in. I was delighted with the physical changes I could see. I also took Adrenocort to suppress the production of testosterone in my body. I don't think I had ever produced much testosterone anyway – I didn't react to things in the same way men do, and my thinking and emotional reactions were always feminine. Everything got softer and womanly. The only way I can describe how I felt about all these changes is that I'd imagine it is like a teenage girl would feel observing her body changes. Being afraid but excited. I felt different. I felt every tablet I took I was losing more and more of Eamon and stepping nearer to completion. I was totally committed to becoming a woman.

1988 was a big year for me – my career was going really well in both London and Dublin, and I flew regularly between both cities. Louis Walsh asked me to go to Amsterdam with the Eurovision team to do the hair and make-up for them all and Johnny Logan won the competition for Ireland for a second time with 'Hold Me Now'. There was one hell of a party after it and I vividly remember sitting in the back room watching the voting and thinking back to the year Dana had won the contest in 1970. I was eleven years of age and Granny wasn't well at the time. I lay at the foot of her bed, which had been moved to the living room of the house, and we watched the Eurovision together.

I was so overawed by the glamour of the whole event I said: "Look, isn't it all so exciting and beautiful! Oh, I'm going to be there some day!"

And Granny laughed and said: "Of course you will, son."

Look at me, folks – it came true!

When we came back to Dublin after the contest I saw the time was right to capitalise on how high my profile had become. I could see a market for high-class models. So the plan that had started to form some years previously when I was working for Robert Chambers came to fruition and I opened Tallon Models in Dublin. I got myself a business partner, a premises, a bank loan, accountants, PA, the lot. Everything legit and up-front, no seediness involved. I was really going to give Tallon Models my all.

It was really only when I began to groom my models, showing them how to walk on a catwalk, how to sit, stand, display a garment, how to do their make-up and how to enhance their beauty that I began to feel yes, yes, this feels right. I was comfortable with the femininity of it all and Rebecca was coming out, with Ross ready to let her shine at this stage.

Business took off like a rocket and we were really pulling in money very fast. We quickly became the top model agency in the country and all the big photographers, fashion designers and magazines looked for Tallon Models. I spent the cash just as fast though. I was at the pinnacle of my career and everyone wanted a piece of me; at a time my head was very messed up.

Ava was almost ten, and although I thought of her daily Andrea was adamant that I couldn't play any role in the child's life. I definitely think I had a few mild depressions in those years, although I never went to a doctor about it, just walked around in a haze, a bubble. Just being. No day or night, morning or evening. A nothingness.

Even then I still wasn't a big drinker. The reason I keep mentioning drink is that it still baffles me how I got to where I ended up, how I became dependent on alcohol of all things – because drink was never a huge part of my life. I was too busy for drink, day and night. As I said, I've always been a night bird – probably because when I lie down to sleep all sorts of unwelcome thoughts, big issues, pop up in that night mode of thinking – you know, where you start to dwell on life in general and your own life in particular. I couldn't lie or sit without myself thinking. I can do it now because I'm at peace without myself, but then I had to be out surrounded by noise and other people – anything to prevent me thinking. I was just hurting back then – through all of my twenties in particular.

10

The Butterfly Emerges

Early in 1989, I was thirty-one and I knew what I had to do. I approached the GP I had been attending since I was a child and told him my feelings about being transgender. I wanted to start legally on the hormone treatments I had been buying illegally in London. I was a basket-case on them and needed something where a medic could monitor me, make sure I was taking the right combinations. I told him I intended to go down that road and eventually seek a gender reassignment operation in London. You had to be on the hormones and also prove that you had been living as a woman for a considerable period of time in order for the surgical team in London to agree to operate. The operation was not available in Dublin. None of this is something anyone goes into lightly. Apart from the six-hour operation, there is a complete hormone rebalancing and psychiatric programme to be gone through. Then there is the whole social stigma and lack of acceptance in wider society to be addressed.

I did not decide to do all these things on a whim. I battled long and hard with myself. But by this stage I had started to hate my male body. My 'male bits'– I even hate the proper names for them and never ever use the words if I can avoid it – actually made me feel physically sick. I avoided looking at or touching them as much as possible. If I wore tight-fitting clothes I would tape them down between my legs with packing tape. The pain of pulling that off was excruciating – but I loathed this most obvious physical sign of gender. Once I knew I could get rid of them, it became the only possibility. It was either that or my sanity.

The GP didn't do me any favours. Perhaps he was old-fashioned or not up to date on all the possibilities but he rang my mum after I left him – there's ethical for you – and a family powwow was called yet again to 'discuss Eamon'. Without Eamon being there of course. I got it into my head that they would attempt to put me into a mental institution. I wasn't mad, just messed up physically. So I did what I always do, escaped to London leaving the agency in charge of my business partner and his girlfriend.

I went to a doctor in London, who put me in touch with a clinic who would assess me and monitor my progress. The clinic got me onto a psychiatric programme in one of the three London hospitals that deal with 'Gender Identity Dysphoria'. I was rigorously questioned and examined every time I attended. They gave me a proper prescription for hormones, but I was still loop de loop on them. I discovered years later that one of the hormones – Adrenocort – was the drug that was actually given to rapists in prisons to suppress their sexual appetites. I was completely wired on the bloody things. PMT on speed.

The combination of oestrogen and male hormone suppressants certainly made me feel more female and I finally started to sprout little boobs! Tiny little things but they were mine, all my own. I had to undergo therapy and see psychologists and they turned my head inside out. I found the process hugely frustrating. I am incredibly impatient. Everything has to be NOW and I determined I was going to have the full operation asap.

Initially I went around as a man in work both at home in Dublin and in London, but dressed androgynously at night when I went to party or to do escort work. The operation was expensive and, although I had a little money coming in from Tallon Models, I wasn't really fit to work clipping hair in London.

I wasn't in great shape physically; I had lost a lot of weight and was down to almost six stone because of the hormones and other drugs (E and cocaine) that I was dabbling in. I had started to drink a lot more alcohol – anything to stop the pain, the pain of being who I was, of being a failed parent, and I felt at times that I was also a failed human being. I did lose faith in God at this time. I even turned my back on my pal the Virgin Mary. But she never abandoned me. For by rights what I put myself through over the next ten years should have

145

killed me, time after time. It was like a howling banshee was running through me all the time.

Then to my horror the press in Dublin started to print terrible stories about me. Because of the weight loss etcetera, a rumour went around that I had contracted AIDS – there was huge fear and lack of information about the virus at that time. I did come back to Dublin for brief periods at this time – don't ask me dates because to be honest I have a very confused recollection of the next twenty years. I have surprised myself at some of the dates I have turned up on documents over the course of writing this book. Sometimes I'm really not sure of what has happened in the blank spots, the blackouts, the lost hours.

I had never paid much attention to what the press said. They had to sell advertising space in newspapers and those of us in the public eye use them as much as they use us. Because the AIDs epidemic was at the height of the news then and because I was outwardly 'gay' and looked like a refugee from a prison camp, people suspected I had contracted the virus; rumours were being spoken of as fact and parents started to pull their daughters from the model agency and move them elsewhere.

The business was really suffering from the bad publicity and worst of all the press started querying my family as to what was going on with me. To protect the family and to save what was left of the business I agreed with my business partner that I should vanish for a while. He knew I was on the hormones, as did my family, and they were all personally supportive. It was hard on them though, particularly my family. They had loved wee Eamon Tallon and had accepted he was now 'gay' Ross Tallon with a broken marriage behind him; now I was telling them I had to let Rebecca become herself. They accepted it but I think they might have preferred if I could have been a little quieter about it! I don't think any of them thought I was fully *compos mentis* though, and I was convinced they would commit me at the first available opportunity.

I blocked out the next decade, perhaps more, of my life – particularly my journey up to my operation – for a long, long time. It was incredibly difficult, very intense, and I have only begun to deal with it over the last two years. I realised I was on the way out of the agency. I couldn't really work at hair and beauty because my hands and eye weren't reliable. I was determined to save the money for the operation myself because I would have to wait too long to have it done on the NHS. I was so close now I was desperate to take the last few steps towards Rebecca. It was a very tough time but I knew this was something I had to do. I would have committed suicide rather than not have the op.

11

Tulip in Amsterdam

Having decided I had to stay away from Dublin, I arrived back in London with £170 in my pocket and a suitcase of clothes at my feet. I remember sitting in Covent Garden and wondering how in the name of God it had it come to this. The day before I had been driving a white convertible Jeep, living in a penthouse apartment and running a thriving business in Dublin. I had blown a fortune in cash, blown out several careers and now really did not know how I was to earn a living. But I was on the road to Rebecca and there was no turning back. She had to be born but she was still some months away and my life seemed incredibly bleak.

I was to stay with Gabriel at his friend's flat initially but when I got there they were out so I climbed in a little window to get into the flat. I felt completely despondent.

I had started to dress occasionally as a woman, but I didn't want to be seen as a transvestite or a drag-queen.

I wanted to be a woman, the woman I was. I was drinking regularly at this stage, and E and cocaine had also become regular parts of my life. Anything to block out the shame and pain of being me and of losing my daughter.

However, you need money for this anaesthetised type of lifestyle.

Gabriel had a gay friend who was heavily involved in the club scene in London and I began to work here and there for him. In fact, this guy had managed some of the bigger nightclubs but he fell out with the owners and set up his own little chain of seedier pubs and rent-boy clubs. I called him Madame Bouffe because he had a big full head of hair which he wore in a bouffant style. In the throes of a row one day with Gabriel, I stormed out and went to Madame Bouffe, asking could I stay with him for a while and he agreed. We actually got on very well and after that I often stayed with him. In fairness, he always put me up if I had nowhere to go. We both loved music and could sit listening to it and chatting about this that and the other for hours. Madame Bouffe had no interest sexually in me although we were of an age – he preferred his lovers to be much younger.

Two guys arrived to stay with Madame Bouffe. One of them was a really lovely Dutch guy – Aalbert was his name and I started going out with him. He was a good ten years younger than me but that didn't seem to bother him. I didn't go out with him for long because I couldn't handle him seeing me as a man. For some reason it has always been younger men that are attracted to me. I hold a fascination for them – curious little boys that they are.

You might say Aalbert was the start of my 'younger men' era because my next two serious boyfriends, both of whom I married (at different times obviously!), were also younger than me. Although one was only eleven months my junior, the other was almost fifteen years younger.

Madame Bouffe used to call me his 'prima ballerina' and shifted me around the clubs he was involved in, either as a stripper or as a hostess. It sounds so seedy, doesn't it? But I never felt like that about it. To me it was simply a performance on or off stage. I had pretended to be a man for long enough, so performing as a female on stage was just another make-believe game.

Madame Bouffe was incredibly camp, 'as camp as a row of tents' as they say, and amused any of my family who met him no end. Once Mum and her friend Hetty came over to visit me and I (stupidly) arranged to meet them down near the strip club I was working in. I got all the other strippers to hang around outside the club hiding the posters which showed it was a strip joint! Mum had a beautiful pink jump-suit on her that day. Even though she was in her fifties she still had a great figure and could get away with dressing any way she pleased. When Madame Bouffe saw her he admired the suit and said, or rather purred: "My dear," turning her to admire her from all angles, "I must be having that!" The next day before she went back home she dropped over to the club and gave him the suit. Of course Madame Bouffe loved her after that and to this day if I run into him he always asks to be remembered to her.

Gabriel also dabbled in escort work. As I said, I

actually have no idea how he earned a living. Every time
I'd meet him he'd have a different job or a different
boyfriend or sugar daddy. He was always well-dressed and
never seemed to get sucked into anything too seedy – at
least on the surface. He minded himself. I think his
background must have been somewhat dysfunctional from
little things he would say. But he never really opened up to
me. I wonder if he has ever opened up to anyone.

Vodka was my drink of choice – because someone
said it doesn't smell. Liar. It does if you drink so much
of it that it's oozing out of your pores. I was a daily
drinker and gradually becoming more dependent on it –
but still didn't see it as a problem. Gabriel drank with
me but he was more of a binge drinker – he'd go on a
three-day bender and then he wouldn't drink for about
six weeks. We would go out together and cruise Soho,
basically looking for someone to buy us drink.

I worked for a while behind the bar Madame Bouffe
ran in Gerrard Street. New Year's Eve was approaching.
Madame Bouffe had been on at me to dress as a woman
for the New Year's Eve party. I didn't want to do it. I
had gone out the odd time in female clothing, but
nothing as public as a large party. I remember thinking
'*Well, if I don't pull it off then I can always pretend I
was doing drag – having a laugh.*' I took great pains
with my make-up and accessories and I can still vividly
see what I wore – a crushed, deep green velvet dress that
came to the knee, a pair of winkle-picker, stiletto shoes
and a brown, bobbed wig. Even if I say so myself, I was
bloody stunning.

I was so nervous walking into that room as 'Pagan' – the name I chose from a book I was reading – but I needn't have been. I was a huge success and I got so much attention that night – and nearly all of it from straight guys – that I was almost crying with delight. It was such a roaring success that I vowed never, ever, ever again to dress as a man. I remember thinking *'I wonder would Ava accept me?'*, then pushing the thought to the back of my mind – it was too much to deal with.

The only time I would temporarily abandon my female persona after that was if I had to come back to Ireland for any reason. I would dress androgynously and tone down my make-up on these occasions.

Rebecca was taking control – at last. All during this period I was attending the hospital and, as I said, was on a particular programme with psychologists and psychiatrists assessing my suitability for surgery. Three different psychiatric teams had to fully assess me and agree I had 'Gender Identity Dysphoria' – GID. I've been teased that I was going from gay to giddy – but there was nothing funny about it. Thinking about it and seeking out a surgeon to operate and remove my hated 'male bits' and tidy me away neatly with the female bits hidden as they should have been was intensely wearing. Sometimes it would all get too much for me and I would feel like running a thousand miles away.

One evening Gabriel came in and suggested that we both go to Amsterdam with Aalbert and the other Dutch lad, both of whom were travelling there that night. I don't know what space my head was in or what drugs or alcohol I had taken but all of a sudden it seemed like a supremely good idea. We travelled by coach on the ferry and I don't remember any formalities like customs or anything. I have the funny feeling that what the guys were doing might not have been the most legal pursuit in the world. But I asked no questions, just looked the other way if I saw something I didn't particularly want to see.

God, I was truly insane at that time! Drink was playing a huge part in my life and that, on top of steroids and other drugs, was enough to make me more than a little 'tired and emotional'. I was also probably co-dependent on Gabriel. He fascinated me at the time – not in any sexual way – but, I don't know, he was like a little devil whispering in my ear. "Come on, come on – just try it!" So I did what I always did – let myself be led.

We landed in Amsterdam, in the seediest part of town, and were put up in this horrible little black room with three or four guys and when I came fully to my senses I really wasn't sure how I'd got there. The place seemed to belong to a British man, let's call him Morgan, and I realised pretty quickly that the place I was staying, the only place I had to stay, was part of a building that was a male brothel by day and a drinking den by night. The only other time I'd been in Amsterdam was when I had gone over with the Johnny Logan Eurovision contingent. It was certainly a completely different experience to the upmarket spaces I'd been in last time over there.

I don't know what it is about me, whether it's because I'm a Gemini or impatient or just a perfectionist. But no matter where I end up I have this remarkable knack of ending up 'in charge'. So there I am – not sure of date, year (almost planet) – but I'm in Amsterdam – halfway between Ross and Rebecca – and I became madam of Morgan's brothel.

My previous dabbles with E and cocaine increased. I was using daily and I was in a very dark place in my head. Physically I looked horrible. I was so thin and although little breasts had budded with the hormones, they were very little – it was chicken fillets in the bra. And I still had bloody horrible dangly male bits, even though they were almost always taped out of sight. So what does Eamon/Ross-on-the-way-to-Rebecca do? What Eamon/Ross/Rebecca back then always did: worked, danced, drank, talked, listened to music and took anything chemical to hand in a bid to blot out the demons running around and around in my head.

I knew this brothel/illegal drinker was not a good place to be – but I was totally incapable of making any decision for myself at the time. I just followed the crowd. Laughing, 'Yeah, yeah, is that right, yeah'. Numbing my fear with whatever was to hand. So I performed – everyone loved me – good old trannie, dressed mostly in swimsuits, wigs, high heels and tights – swanning about the place, a great performer, always good for a laugh. And I was cringing inside.

I was in Amsterdam for about eight months and I had very little contact with my family or any of my

London friends over this period. I was totally isolated and I think this is the time that my life started to totally spin out of control. Of the group of us that hung about together, someone would have cash and we'd buy a bag of coke from Danzer up the road. My drinking continuously increased – sometimes to bring me down gently from the drugs. I worked through nearly every night and would sleep for a few hours in the mornings. Then I'd get myself done up and go out to the Haymarket area of Amsterdam, to shop and visit a church. Clothes and the Virgin Mary – I was on speaking terms with her again – my two sanctuaries, all my life. I could lose myself in clothes shopping – it was definitely my first dependency – if I was in a shop I could quite happily wander about for hours, lose myself in the clothes and shoes, concentrate on the outward appearance and totally bury the screaming frightened child inside and all my woes. Or so I thought. You cannot bury this stuff though. That, I eventually discovered.

The I.T. club was a popular watering hole for the fashionable people of Amsterdam and when it closed at 3 a.m. people in the know would spill down to the area where the brothel was. Morgan operated it as a male brothel by day and a late-night drinking den at night, and myself as hostess looked after all the punters. What they wanted they got. I smoothed paths for everyone, talking, laughing, flirting: like a cocktail waitress – all glammed up, wearing outfits similar to those worn by the Playboy girls. I made sure the punters bought overpriced drinks and enjoyed themselves. It would be well into the day before they would all go home to wherever home was – then probably all come out the next night and repeat the process. It was a seedy, sleazy part of the world and I was right in the thick of it.

The brothel was just a couple of steps away from a canal and around there little drinking dens kept opening and closing all the time. The crowds would move from one to the other.

The brothel, like all the clubs, had security guys working on the door and these guys were really tough – they looked scary enough to prevent most trouble. One night, or rather morning, shortly after the last customers had left, I heard screams and shouts coming from the small room off the bar. This was where the security guards would sit and keep an eye open for trouble and they often used it as a place to rest between shifts to play cards and drink if the place was quiet. On this occasion they had been having a few drinks, it had been a busy night and everyone was tired.

Then Morgan came out of the room and told me to open the door out to the street and to check if there was anyone about. He was carrying a baseball bat with blood on it and his shirt was covered in blood – from the look in his eye I didn't question him. My mouth dried anyway, I wouldn't have been able to ask him anything. I just did what I was told. The coast was clear and I called back to him that everything was okay. Morgan and three other men came from the security guards' room carrying a young Turkish man who had been working in the club. He had been badly beaten up and was covered in blood, his face bruised and swollen. It took me a minute to recognise him. I felt sick. They carried the boy past me with Morgan roaring, 'Get in there, *you*! Clean that room – *now*!' at me as they passed.

They threw the boy in the canal. I heard the splash. I was terrified in case he was dead and I didn't find out until the following day that he had dragged himself out of the Amstel and disappeared to safety. The poor guy was an illegal immigrant and I heard that, because of that, he was afraid to go to the police. I was paralysed with fear but I did as I was told. You don't mess with these men – they are seriously dangerous, placing no value on anyone's life. I got a bucket of hot water and a mop and some cloths and I gagged when I opened the door of the room. There was a pool of deep red blood on the floor, and blood spattered on the furniture and way up on the walls. I can remember the terror in my soul as I cleaned and I saw the water in the bucket turn pink then red then a deeper brownish colour. I was shaking so much I quite honestly could hardly use the mop. But not using it, not doing what Morgan told me to do, would have meant my blood would have been splashed on the other wall. I did the best I could. I think I changed that water a dozen times. It was a few days before one of the men got quite drunk and told me the reason why Morgan had beaten the young man up. They had sent him to bring them some bottles of beer and on his way back in the lad stumbled and dropped one of the bottles of Amstel and the lager splashed Morgan's trousers. So Morgan picked up a baseball bat, that was always handy in that room, and using it and his feet he beat the living daylights out of the boy.

It was the talk of the area for the next week, all whispers, in corners of course, everyone fearful, afraid to open their mouths or look crooked at any of the men who had been in that room. No police ever came and I never reported it. What could I report? Some unnamed immigrant boy was beaten up by four men who would not hesitate to call me a liar and kill me when I left the police station? I often wonder about that boy, wonder was there anything I could have done. I pray to God he made his way home to his family.

I can see now how seedy, dreadful and amoral it all was. But at the time I was living hand to mouth. The money I was getting from Tallon Models was inconsequential – but, as I wasn't there putting work into the agency, I could hardly expect profits from it. I wasn't doing well-paid London stripping or escort work and only had my wages from Morgan's brothel/club. I worked long hours for that money and Morgan wasn't the most generous employer in the world. I was terrified the whole time. I didn't run. I wasn't able to and if I had been able I wouldn't have known where to run to. I was afraid to go home to Granard or to Dublin – even London seemed threatening to me, too close to home, although I was waiting all the time to be called back there for my operation.

I'd ring Mum or my cousin Mary every so often and

pretend everything was great, that I was living a life of luxury, doing hair and make-up for fashionable people and had lots of friends. Instead I was living a life that would make anyone cringe.

But I just got on with it. I had to. I had to eat and at that time it was the only way I felt I could earn money. My prescriptions had run out and I had to source my hormones and was also spending any spare cash I had on cocaine at this stage too. Any post-op transgender will tell you that this transition period is the hardest part. Every day you open your eyes it seems impossible to keep going. But I did. I don't know what drove me. I think now it was probably my faith. I would talk to Our Lady in my head, asking her for forgiveness and for guidance. I still wasn't fully reconciled with God or Jesus, but Our Lady was a woman and a mother of sorts to me and I always got comfort from talking to her.

I did meet some really good people in Amsterdam. A lot of male and female prostitutes come from broken, dysfunctional backgrounds which makes them more vulnerable to both addiction or mental-health problems. Men like Morgan see these vulnerablities and exploit them. Prostitution was the easiest way for a lot of these unfortunate men and women to put food in their mouths, booze in their bellies or drugs up their nose or in their arms. To state the obvious, prostitutes were once babies too but somehow, somewhere, things went awry for them. They shouldn't have to justify themselves to anyone but themselves and they generally don't bother. It is a job. Like most of the rest of the world they do what they have to do to survive. Like me. I had to be the biggest, the noisiest, the most glamorous madam – anything to hide and protect the trembling little girl within.

In my time in Amsterdam, I also met some of the women who were working Amsterdam's infamous windows. Many of these girls were well-educated, one was even a teacher, and they did this to get money for one reason or another. Usually to support family in another part of Europe or to pay college fees.

After that incident in the brothel with the Turkish boy, Morgan moved me on to another club a friend of his was involved in, in a more salubrious part of the city. This one wasn't sleazy at all, actually it was quite upmarket; a spiral staircase led up to the club and I suppose the nicest way of describing it is that it was a type of cocktail club or hostess bar for gay men. It was a pick-up joint really, and some of the guys would be escorts on the payroll. These boys were always very, very handsome and they would entertain the punters by stripping or dancing.

This club wasn't a brothel and whatever the escorts did with the customers when they were clocked off was their own affair. Although knowing Morgan and his friends, I'd be surprised if he hadn't set up a lot of these 'dates' and got his cut directly from the escorts if they indulged the customers.

I just tried to keep quiet and as out of trouble as I could but really I was a train-crash waiting to happen. Anyone who has gone through any type of experience where they feel they do not have the upper hand, where they are being exploited because of their weakness, whatever their experience might be, will tell you, you close your mind down, go into auto-pilot and do what you have to do to survive. If I could survive repeated rape as a small child, I could take some serious abuse as a grown woman.

Even in the bowels of Amsterdam I found good, decent friends – intelligent people to hang out with, and they were totally accepting of me. I would discuss my gender reassignment with them and perhaps for the first time I began to articulate how I had felt over the course of my lifetime. I think it was to one of these girls, Heidi, that I spoke first of the abuse I had suffered as a child. She was great – we would talk for hours about it and slowly she made me see that I was not to blame for any of that. I had been a child – a little boy who was already confused because he felt like a girl. Then that little girl terrified inside a little boy was dragged away from the security of home and placed in an institution run entirely by men and containing only males, and then confused even more because of being sexualised at such an early age. Heidi was better than any counsellor and put me in touch with other post-op transgender women. They too were supportive, and my determination and feeling that the operation was my only salvation grew and grew.

My self-esteem started to rise again. I'd think to myself, '*I'm better than this. I owe myself more than this*', and I also knew that living the way I was would definitely mean never seeing Ava again. I knew I couldn't stay in this hovel of a life any longer but I thought to myself, *'I'm on the right path – I know for the first time ever that I'm doing the right thing'.*

Tallon Models was doing well in Ireland and my partner contacted me to say that he wanted to take over the business completely. I did come back to Dublin for a month or two after my Amsterdam stint to tie up the loose ends of Tallon Models. I found it really hard to let it go; I hated looking at shots of models and realising they could have been my models.

While I was home I earned a few bob by managing a nightclub in Leeson Street called Chaos. The owner had asked me if I could liven it up a bit. I remember him commenting that the only thing chaotic about it was its name – it was dead at a time when all the other clubs in Leeson Street were hopping. He thought I might do the club a world of good. I was still Ross in Dublin although I was already well on the road to Rebecca, but the persona I used in the club was more like the character I used to front the drinking den in Amsterdam. The money Chaos was offering was good and I thought a few months of it would tide me over until I went back to London. I needed to keep building my operation money – having a drug and drink 'habit' makes saving cash a little difficult.

Ecstasy was fast becoming the drug of choice on Dublin's club scene then and in order to perform as

Eamon (left) & siblings, Granard National School, circa 1964

Eamon (right) on his Communion Day, Granard, with his brother

Lucy & Eamon at the Corner House (now demolished), Granard, circa 1964

Eamon (right) & brother, Granard, circa 1964 (note the one roller-skate!)

Lucy's Communion Day, Granard. Eamon & brother, local postman,
Uncle Jack and cousin Cathy

Seated left to right: Eamon, his first girlfriend Lorraine, Lucy & friend.
Standing left to right: Aunty Maureen, Uncle Pat & Mum (Circa 1975)

Ross as male model, 1983 Photos by Brendan Bourke
www.brendanbourke.ie

Ross polaroid shot by Shane McCarthy (testing lighting for photo shoot 1983)
www.shanemccarthy.ie

Ross with dance srtiste from Hot Gossip, at Rolling Stone Bill Wyman's wedding 1989

Bill Wyman & Mandy Smith at their wedding 1989

Ross with Mandy at Wyman/Smith wedding 1989 (He did the hair & make-up)

May I kiss the bride? Bill, Ross & Mandy

The Rolling Stones at the Wyman/Smith wedding 1989

Rebecca in early recovery after surgery in London. Photos by Hannah Grace Deller
www.hannahdeller.com

Rebecca in the *Sunday World*, 1994.
Photo by Val Sheehan

Rebecca, Golden Square, London, February
1st 2008. Photo by Hannah Grace Deller
www.hannahdeller.com

Current shots of Rebecca. Taken by Shane McCarthy: www.shanemaccarthy.ie

hostess in Chaos I was running on E more than anything else. I went to the club at 10p.m. or 11p.m. at night, dressed in swimsuits and fishnet stockings, hair in a ponytail and went around as 'Miss Whiplash'. I got the punters in and I did turn the club around in a short time, but, Christ, I paid for it.

This was only a brief period – maybe two or three months but it often feels like a lot longer. In fact, and I don't think this is drink or drugs distorting things, a lot of the things I have done in my life can seem like that. Intense, like I have to pack everything into this tiny window of opportunity. I do nothing half-heartedly – I don't think I am capable of that. It's always all or nothing with me. I wouldn't get out of Chaos until maybe six or seven in the morning because I wouldn't have gone home when the club closed. I was too wired to sleep anyway. I might have a few drinks in the club after clean-up or go to an early house for a few drinks with some of the staff. I permanently looked trashed – just from the lifestyle I was leading, wearing drag make-up and doing a long shift where I had to be this raucous, fun-loving lunatic. Going home to bed in a taxi with make-up caked in, dressed in a swimsuit, a coat and precious little else. I hated this life. But nobody would employ me unless I was this tramp, this bitch, a cartoon creation. I would get in from the club and scrub – literally scrub – every part of my body to wash away that creation.

My body clock, which had never followed any ordinary pattern anyway, refused to settle completely into that of a night-shift worker. I still wanted to hang

onto my daytime life, so I might sleep for four hours
and then get dressed up and go into the city around
lunchtime. I still wanted to do a whole normal daytime
existence; shop, talk to friends etcetera. I had to keep
going, wear myself out – run from my thoughts.
Something had to give.

The same type of press coverage as I'd been subject
to in the previous year started to appear in the papers
once again. I knew I couldn't stay in Ireland on a fulltime basis and I doubted Ireland would ever accept me.
I was dressing as a woman all the time now and the
press had got hold of my intended sex-change operation, I
suppose because my business had such a high media
profile. I also was never the quietest person in the city,
but I really felt that at that time I was bloody hounded
out of the country. They never left me alone and I had
family too who were being affected by this.

So there I was, someone who had always courted
publicity for the sake of business, irritated beyond belief
by being unable to go anywhere without someone taking
my picture or printing the most unbelievable untruths
about me. The paparazzi were constantly seeking Andrea
and Ava too, but as I had no contact with them they could
not be found through me and were therefore protected
from the media attention. I vowed I would never come
home for any length of time again as the stories about
me meant that family members were getting really badly
hurt. London would be home for me from then on out.

12

Welcome to the World . . . Baby Girl

When I look back on that period in Amsterdam it is
with a sense of horror. It really was a twilight sort of
existence. Neither Ross nor Rebecca were there – it was
this lunatic Pagan/madam-of-a-brothel that had stalked
the streets. That mad madam could almost be a symbol
for the next fifteen or sixteen years of my life. A crazy
lady in a swimsuit. There were moments, even months,
of lucidity and what passed for normal life over the next
eighteen to twenty years. But a lot of that time was
spent in a hazy half-world of confusion fuelled by drink,
drugs or a combination of both. Forgive me if timelines
appear to overlap or statements appear contradictory. I
have done my best to straighten out the confused tangle
that was to be my life during that period but there were
times when my whole life seemed contradictory. For
example until I started writing this book I could have
sworn I had my gender reassignment in 1991 – in fact,

I had the operation in 1989. My red-letter day and I couldn't remember the year.

It should have had more clarity, for I finally achieved my dream, what I had longed for, albeit not always knowing what it was I longed for since I was a child.

When I returned to London, I went back to the hospital to check on the progress of my case and found I had got the all-clear from everyone who had been assessing me over the years prior to my stint in Amsterdam. They all agreed that my gender was female and I was 'cleared for takeoff'. I could have my operation. I was thrilled. I wanted to have it the day before my 31st birthday in June 1989. I am a romantic and I wanted to be reborn on my birthday and restart my life as the woman I was meant to be.

I debated with friends about what I should call myself. I wanted a name that would see me into older age. Something a little classy and as far away from the vaudeville names I had used in clubs as I could get. I had been toying with 'Amy' as it sounded near enough to Eamon. But at that stage I really hated Eamon and everything he represented. Ross had carried me from Eamon into the woman's body I was finally to get and had done it successfully. I thought I should probably hang onto the 'R' of Ross anyway and considered Ruby or, better, Rachael. Then I thought of Rebecca. It had a certain cachet. I had a horror of walking into a bank in twenty-five years' time, which would put me in my fifties (not that I was ever going to be in my fifties!) and my name being called out: "Chantelle Tallon!" or

'Sabrina' or some other name that would date me or embarrass me.

I was aware at some level that the person I am now – the woman in her fifties that I think has class, the woman that I saw in my soul and the woman I wanted to become, was there. I've ended up the person I wanted to be. I could have done without the journey, mind you, but maybe I wouldn't be as strong as I am if my journey had been different. If I had seen how difficult my path would be in my thirties; a path fuelled by alcohol and drugs and a million mistakes and wrong turnings, and that it would be twenty years before I would be the Rebecca I wanted to be, I don't know if I would have been able to put one foot in front of the other.

Rebecca was a timeless name, a name for every age and so I changed my name to Rebecca Antoinette Tallon by deed poll, and I felt things were finally going my way. But, as usual, it wasn't all plain sailing.

I did have support though – a boyfriend – at that stage in my life. I met him one night in Club Estefano not too long before my operation. I was dancing with my friend Lisa – she too was a pre-op trannie who needed very little to feminise her. She had been caught much earlier than I, luckily for her, and had started hormone treatment in her teens. The medical professions in the UK have been very much to the forefront in pioneering treatment in this field and those of us who have benefited from it are grateful for their efforts. Lisa looked very feminine, a small, curvy, bleached-blonde Essex girl. We were dancing and having fun when this beautiful Brazilian man joined us. He wore a bandana with panache and got away with it – at first I thought he was Italian as he had the same swarthy complexion Mediterranean men have. He tagged along with us all night and when we came back the next night he was there again.

He introduced himself as Stefano Alvarez and he persisted in following me around the clubs for several weeks until I gave in and went out with him. He was very attentive and charming. I told him my whole story and he was completely accepting of me. He cried for me; told me I was so brave. We quickly became an item and before long he had moved in with me. I think the flat I had at that stage was in South Kensington. I can tell you I lived in every postal district in central London over a twenty-year period – and rarely any longer that eight or nine months in any of them. Stefano was a passionate man and our physical relationship initially was very intense. We couldn't get enough of each other, at least until my operation. It was also nice, on a wavelength level, to have someone my own age around as a lot of my friends were in their early twenties – I suppose I was actually in my teens emotionally.

I came home and told Mum and my immediate family about Stefano and of my upcoming operation. They knew I had been living as a woman and had been on hormone treatment. In fact Mum had sent me a Christmas card addressed to Rebecca Tallon which really touched me.

This was the first time I opened up to my family about the sexual abuse I had suffered at the hands of those men in the institution when I was a child. They were all horrified and believed me immediately. It explained a lot of my behaviour to them, how the abuse had tormented me down the years, making me the restless creature I was; jumping from home to home from Billy to Jack, never able to hold down a job or relationship for long, seeking, always seeking, what I thought had been lost to me. Trickles of stories about clerical and institutional sex abuse were starting to appear in the press in Ireland although it would be some years before the full scope of the horror would be uncovered. I still find it extraordinarily difficult, even now – forty-five years after the event – to talk about it. For to talk about it, to write about it, is to relive it. I can still sense them.

Opening up about the abuse was harder than talking about the sex reassignment. I still felt ashamed about it, about letting myself be that abused child, even though I know I could not have prevented it. I am still learning that it was not my fault and I cannot explain the shame, although a lot of victims will tell you of feeling that way too. Perhaps it is because we were children and did not have the vocabulary at the time to articulate what was being done to us nor how we felt about it. I did know when I became 'adult' enough that I was not at fault, never at fault, but a little voice inside me niggled me, telling me I was no good and that's what happened to people who were no good. Will I ever be free of those men? I can still hear their panting, still smell them. I still hate any man standing close behind me – invading my body space.

I had been so afraid my family wouldn't believe me and it was a huge relief to finally talk to them about it. Mum said she was so sorry I had ended up in that school and sorry that she hadn't seen the damage it had done to me. It explained my wilfulness through my teens and early twenties to her. I was a very sad and tortured soul at this stage of my life and my family really, really did their best to help me. Poor old Aunt Sybil, my old helpmate in times of trouble, she cried so much for me. She even took me off on a retreat to a monastery to see could it soothe my troubled mind in any way. I did get a certain amount of peace from it. I had let Our Lady back into my heart already and asked for guidance on the path I was about to embark on.

Talking about the sex reassignment was difficult for some of my family. The males in particular seemed to find it very hard to accept. Funnily, even now decades later, women have no problem accepting me as female but most of the men I meet, once they learn of my 'condition', seem to back off, are afraid or cautious, or maybe just bewildered. I didn't find the subject of my op difficult to talk about because it was for me quite simply a life-saving operation but I really didn't expect anyone else to understand what it was like. I'd had years of misery and confusion, daily praying for deliverance from being imprisoned in my own mismatched body. I just wanted them to accept the fact, accept me no matter what package I came in, that it didn't matter that they thought I was a boy but now knew I was a woman, that I was still the child or sibling I'd always been or the child of their sibling I'd always been. That I was just me, Rebecca. I don't know that anyone can understand how difficult it was, always wanting something, yearning and not knowing for years and years exactly what it was you yearned for.

With Mum's and my family's blessing I set in motion the procedures necessary for my surgery in London. The media in Ireland did get hold of my intention to have a gender reassignment and must have printed something about it, because one day I rang Lucy and she told me that her daughter Eleanor, who was very young, was being teased about me in the school yard. Lucy was living in Granard with her husband and her children went to the National School I had gone to for my first few years.

"Your Uncle Eamon – is he a man or a woman?" was the cat-call in the playground.

Quick as a flash Eleanor turned her head and said, "I don't know – but his name is Rebecca."

I was delighted – if Eleanor could love me and stick up for me, and my mother, siblings, aunts could accept me, well, maybe there was hope for Ireland yet.

The surgery wasn't a decision I took lightly, a whim – "Ah, I think I'll become a woman today" – it was not a fashion statement or some must-have accessory. I had taken a life-time of agonising to accept what I was, the feeling that it was the only path for me growing from my mid-twenties to this point. It had to be done. It was as life-saving an operation as replacing a diseased heart or a diseased pair of lungs. I was to spend six hours in the operating theatre and I had been warned of all the risks of not pulling through. I had been diagnosed as asthmatic in my late twenties and an anaesthetic for any asthmatic is dodgy, but an asthmatic who had been smoking, drinking in smoky pubs and clubs and dabbling with drugs? I was high risk, but for me there was no decision to make – if I didn't have it done I would be dead anyway – because Rebecca could not live in Eamon/Ross's body any longer. People ask, "What did it feel like, being a woman in the wrong body?" I don't know, is the answer, because I never had the luxury of being in the right body from day one to compare it with. It's like asking someone what's it like being left-handed (which I am). You can't describe it. It just is.

One thing I'd like to mention here is that all the psychiatrists I have had to meet and talk to, over and over again, said that my gender 'issue' would most probably have arisen whether I had been sexually abused as a child or not. It is thought that gender is decided in the hypothalamus area of the brain in the first three months after conception. Long before genitalia are formed. Maybe paedophiles sense something more vulnerable in people like me and use that to their advantage. It is a discussion for another day, a long and very sad discussion.

My life in London was busy, I was working at whatever I could, hair, make-up, I did as little as the escort work as I could because my mood swings were huge and I would not have made a good job of being eye candy on someone's arm. This escorting didn't bother Stefano – he was possessive but not when it came to this. I can see now that he liked the money it brought; he was not the most industrious person I have ever met.

I also had a list of personal clients whose hair I looked after. I ensured my hand and eye were steady enough to do what I was best at – in fact, with a certain level of toxicity in my body I could function perfectly, and I could, and did, command any fee. These were wealthy people and the jobs always paid well. These clients would recommend me to other women and I could get bookings to go to clients' houses the morning of a wedding or big occasion. These days were really well paid, but I was also partying hard as was Stefano.

My weekends fell into a pattern of a two-and-a-half-day binge of clubs, booze, E and cocaine. The club scene in London was huge in the early 90s – Trade, the Hippodrome, Stringfellows, Turnmills, Heaven – all the beautiful people were there from the world of high fashion, beauty, media and the arts. All dancing, drugging, drinking. A standard weekend for me then consisted of the following. We – myself, Stefano, and whatever group of friends we happened to be with, it was a group that changed constantly – would all meet in one person's flat on a Friday evening and drink vodka and down E's or whatever was to hand as we got ready for a weekend of clubbing. Although I had taken E sporadically up to this, my usage increased. I wouldn't have considered myself as a big 'E-head' at that stage, although Stefano was, and I would still gag swallowing half a tab with a drink of vodka. But once it was down I was ready to dance the night away.

We would start in one club, say Heaven – one of the group would nearly always have their name on the guest list of one or another of the more popular clubs. Remember, I knew almost all the top models, photographers and make-up artists in both the UK and Ireland then. Media and artistic people tended to be around too. People would actually jet into London to party and be seen partying, so there was always some group we could tag along with. When Heaven closed at half three or four we would then go on to Trade in Farringdon until they threw us out at about two the following afternoon, bleary-eyed as the zombies in Michael Jackson's *Thriller*, into the sedate world of Saturday shoppers.

We would go and chill for a few hours in someone's house, smoking a little ganga to help bring us down from the E, maybe doze a little – there was rarely any food involved – then get ready again and go on to Club Estefano, then on to Turnmills, and back to Trade or to a late-night drinker. We would spill onto the street in bright daylight at 8a.m. Monday morning as suited and booted financial London was making its way to work. It was a bitch in the summer – the glare would nearly blind you.

"Aw' righ', darlin'!" we'd shout at the prim and proper office workers scurrying off to their nine-to-fives as we crawled out and danced our way to our personal hells. We thought they were all so sad, that they had no lives.

I had a rough reminder of this in December 2009. I was back in London for a few days and I was out walking across the city at 8a.m. on a Sunday morning. I spotted a gaggle of well-dressed, noisy young people in their early twenties all crowding into a club on Saville Row. I could almost see myself in them and I felt so glad that part of my life is past me. My heart ached for them and I hope to God they come through the experience unscathed.

As I led this crazy social life I was saving all the time for my sex reassignment operation. I often look back and wonder how I didn't just implode under the strain of it all. It was certainly chaotic but then I hadn't known anything but chaos since I was seven years of age.

There were two types of surgical sex reassignment on offer – there was an important difference between them. Some wit had christened the cheaper of the operations – at £5,000 – as the 'Brighton Fanny': cheap and cheerful. The other operation cost £6,995 and had the added benefit of more effort being made to minimise nerve damage, thus ensuring that I could still achieve an orgasm. For those of you who want the gory details, diagrams etc, try the internet or any of the transgender groups scattered about the world. I didn't even want to know at the time how they remodelled me. I just wanted rid of the three-piece suite – a corner unit was my preference. I have provided a list of websites at the back of the book that will give the anatomical details.

I still don't understand why it didn't cost the even seven thousand. Was it a special offer or something? Maybe they thought you would tip the surgeon that last fiver! Of course I wanted the best – I freely admit to being high-maintenance. Rebecca had waited long enough – she was going to get the best.

The surgeon was a lovely man, the best in his field – a Mr Dalrymple, and I was booked in for my operation in London Bridge Hospital the day before my birthday. So when I woke up on June 6th I would be a woman – a proper one, not buried in a male body.

I had to pay for 50% of the operation upfront, which meant saving as much of the cash I made as I could, and as I was also partying hard I needed money for socialising, drink and looking good, as did my boyfriend who I was keeping at this stage. I did whatever bit of modelling and hair and make-up styling that came my way.

I had applied for a Council flat and my name was on the Housing List. In the United Kingdom if you are transgender you are classified as 'disabled' and instead of unemployment benefit you can claim disability benefit. This is because, in general, transgender people have difficulty finding work – employers just don't want to know. I was lucky to be talented and self-employed and still reasonably in demand. I was still able to pick and choose work by day. It was to be 1994 before I actually claimed any disability benefits. I needed the cash faster than clipping hair could get it so I looked for more escort work.

One of my escort clients was a lovely man of whom I became very fond. He was quite wealthy and at the time had a magnificent flat off the Bayswater Road. This is in a very beautiful area of London very near Hyde Park. He was a regular client and two or three evenings a week I would keep him company over dinner and then we would go back to his flat on the Bayswater road. He was lonely, I think, and I made him laugh. Mostly I'd listen to him talk. I was fond of him. I never slept with him although I would have if he'd wanted to because I had developed a fondness for him. But sex was not what that man wanted. I think I just fascinated him.

I was expensive though – I was paid £200 an hour and that was after the agent's cut – and I might be with this man, let's call him Charles, for two or three hours. He liked to look at me, talk to me and I would keep him company as he drank. I could have freeloaded drink as much as I liked then, but this was a career – high-class escorting is a business – and the one thing you don't do in work is get drunk. Of course the drunker you could get the client the more you could get out of them: '*Fools and their money are soon parted.*' There was a gang of us escorts that would meet up regularly and compare notes. I do know some escorts slept with the clients but most of us didn't. It's a bit like being a therapist. Most of the people who use agencies are not looking for anything other than companionship – and for whatever reason they seem unable to find it any other way. They want someone to give them time who is not looking for anything other than a day's pay – no emotional attachment or baggage – and I had plenty of time to give them. I am a good listener and I can empathise with people – I can also make them laugh. There are strict rules when you're in that game. You do not talk about your family or personal life and do not ask the client questions about their family unless they lead you into it. If a client wants to talk about his family he will do what the rest of us do, ring his mother. So you might admire something he's wearing or flatter him. A superficial generalised kind of conversation. That's why the client is hiring you. Someone to listen to him, to make him feel good.

I got to know Charles quite well and one evening in his flat he said, "Your eyes look very unhappy."

"Are they?" I answered. I thought I could cover everything up with a veneer of make-up and a false smile.

"Yes," he said. "There is a blackness in them – they look like they should be a different colour. Like they don't fit – they're glazed over – it's like you're hiding in there."

He was perceptive. My eyes wouldn't have been glazed from drink or drugs at that stage but unhappiness shines out of one's eyes, doesn't it?

Then I broke the house rule and said "Yes, I suppose I am unhappy sometimes."

"Is there anything I could give you to make you happy?" he asked.

At this stage I had tiny little breasts, about a 32A and would wear a WonderBra with socks pushed into it. It felt like a haversack on the wrong way around. It drove me mad. I know it was superficial – I had plenty of other things to bother me. But to me and anyone else who is third gender, body appearance is crucially important.

I can be blunt and to the point so I quipped, "I'd love tits for breakfast!"

"Okay," he laughed. "I'll pay for them – on one condition – that I can be the first one to see them when they're done!"

"No problem," I said.

I didn't think he was serious but when I was leaving he repeated the offer and told me to make the appointment. He had probably just handed me £1,000 for sitting with him amusing him for hours.

I decided to go along for a consultation before my big op – to get a price so I could report back to Charles and maybe book myself in as a pick-me-up treat after I was anatomically correct down below, like taking a car to a mechanic and asking for a written estimate! I went to a consultant in Harley Street known in the 'sisters' community as 'The Titman'. I paid for the consultation myself and we discussed it and I told him I'd like at least a 'C' cup. He didn't think there would be any problem and I asked when they could be done – I had a date for my sex reassignment operation and wondered could I have both ops done around the same time. I thought it would be marvellous to have the whole package together. The Titman told me he could do the job in the next couple of days so I asked him to hang on for a minute and I went out to Reception and rang Charles.

"Do you remember you said you'd buy me tits for breakfast?"

"Yes."

"Well, I'm here in Harley Street and the consultant says he can do them in the next few days."

"I have the credit card here," he said. "Hand me over to the receptionist."

He gave her the details and that was it. Done deal!!! I was so thrilled I went and celebrated for forty-eight hours.

I had the breast enlargement done the following week. When I came round after the surgery I groggily looked downwards and, because there was a good deal of bruising and swelling, initially I thought my new boobs were enormous and between that and the post-op grogginess I started to shriek, "Oh my God! I can't see past them!" The nurses had a great giggle with me – once they calmed me down – honestly, the tits were so swollen I could have breastfed myself. But when the pain and swelling went I thought they were magnificent. There was some tiny scarring which a man on a flying horse wouldn't notice and I was over the moon, I was truly on my way to a female body. I had boobs!!

People would ask me how much my boob job had cost and I could say, "I think they were about three grand. I don't know, a man friend paid for them."

I'm afraid I didn't keep my side of the bargain.

Stefano got first viewing after myself and, although Charles got to look, he didn't get to touch.

"Oh no! They're too sore," I exclaimed as his hand drew near.

He just laughed. I think he really loved giving me the pleasure of my breasts.

I flaunted those boobs as soon as I could. I loved them and went around wearing the lowest tops I could get away with. I even had to buy a support bra! Stefano was getting quite possessive of me at this stage and, although he loved me to look well on his arm, we did row about the neckline of some of my more 'OTT' tops!

My sex reassignment operation was booked for about two months after the breast enlargement. I was two thousand pounds short of the balance due and I was terrified I was going to have to cancel. A post-op trannie friend, Nikki, said she would help me out – she would lend me the cash. I was thrilled. I was due to go into the hospital on a Sunday and have the operation on a Monday so I arranged to meet Nikki on the Friday one week before the due date to get the cash from her. She never showed. I waited for ages, phoned her place but to no avail. I couldn't track her down. She had quite simply changed her mind.

I rang the hospital and told them I wouldn't have the money. I was gutted; I had been so built up for this, this finally getting the body I wanted. All my friends were shocked at Nikki changing her mind – she of all people should have realised how vulnerable I was at that stage. Luckily another friend stepped into the breach and, although I couldn't have the operation the day before my birthday as I had hoped, I actually ended up having it a few days early! At least I had it in my birth month. Because of the confusion in cancelling and rebooking the operation, the procedure was actually carried out in the beautiful Portland Hospital, a private hospital in Weymouth Street, W1.

I was in bits after the operation and in a lot of pain.

When I came to I had one question only, "Is it gone?"

Stefano was smiling at me and he nodded, yes, as I drifted back into unconsciousness, happy.

The bruising, swelling and initial scarring in the groin area were not a pretty sight. But the medical staff were fantastic, and were all so kind and sensitive in dealing with me, I loved them all. Gradually it all subsided and I was thrilled. The hated male genitalia were gone. I was all neat and feminine and tucked away. Despite all I had been through, the pain and bewilderment and seediness, I felt great hope. I felt I could start life afresh, forge ahead and be happy. Above all be happy. I thought of my daughter, who was heading into her teens, becoming a woman herself. I cried a little for her and hoped her path would be smooth and happy. I wondered how she would feel about me now if she knew. I hoped above all that she was surrounded by people who loved her and who would help her through any dark days that might come her way.

I did push Ava to the back of my mind a lot of the time; I had to in order to survive. I cannot explain to what lengths I went to gain access to her without hurting other people. Suffice it to say I adored her. When I lived with her and Andrea, I carried Ava with me all the time. But the world was a different place then. It seems Victorian – Neanderthal even – looking now at attitudes then. Ava was never ever forgotten. But I thought I would never be part of her life and I couldn't brood on it. I would have gone insane with ifs, ands, buts and maybes.

I was assigned a social worker in the hospital to help me readjust to the world as a female. London really looked after me in this regard and I have a lot to thank the British Social Services and Health Services for. Although I paid for the operation privately, I could have had it done on the NHS if I had been prepared to wait. England looked after me when the Irish system wouldn't even acknowledge me. London was truly Rebecca's birthplace. As far as I was concerned I was reborn, or rather born correctly, there. Whole and clean and in the right body.

I disappeared off the club scene for a couple of months, but as I was wont to up sticks and disappear to Dublin or to other cities around Europe every so often I don't think anyone noticed. I do remember being very lonely at times and wondering, 'Is this it? I've got what I always wanted and I'm still not satisfied?' The truth of the matter was that my operation hadn't brought the automatic happiness and fulfilment I had expected it to. But it would be many painful years before I had the self-knowledge to realise that there would be no true happiness until I faced my inner demons. I wondered could I ever be happy? Had I the capacity for happiness? I genuinely did not realise until the very recent past that I was, and always have been, responsible for my own happiness. Like many pubescent children I expected happiness to be conferred on me by something outside of myself.

Stefano was there but we had started fighting a lot. Our sex life was sporadic, not least because it was bloody painful, and I had a lot of issues still to deal with. I would often feel so alone – that's the worst kind of loneliness, the one you feel when you're in a relationship. But I desperately needed him at that time. To see me and treat me as the complete woman I had finally become. I suppose I was clinically depressed but I didn't go to the doctor. I have never been able to do silence or being alone. I have never done it since my days in the institution: silence and being alone meant being joined by someone unpleasant back then. There were some very bleak moments for me and I used the vodka bottle as too much of a crutch during this time. I think up to this I had used alcohol as a social lubricant, Dutch courage etcetera, but I think it is probably during this time that my dependency on alcohol, my need for it to block out feelings first started.

It must have been several months after the operation before I felt brave enough to face the world again. Which I did with my usual bang, of course. A 'Page 3' spread. Having been a stripper, being naked in front of people didn't bother me and I had waited so long and had pined so much for this body, this beautiful Rebecca, that I wasn't hiding her light under a bushel. She was going to brazenly shine to the world. I went to the *Sunday World* and did a 'Page 3' photo-shoot for both England and Ireland. I had landed. It was as if an enormous weight had been lifted off my shoulders and now I could float or fly, go where I pleased, be who I wanted to be. I had waited and put up with being rejected and feeling hunted and now I was ready to say: "Well, fuck you – all of you! Look at me! I'm here – a real, live beautiful woman!"

13

Love and Marriage – Part Deux

I was in my thirties, a time when most people are settling down, secure in relationships and careers, and thinking about building homes and families for themselves, but psychologically I was a young teenager. As I said, sex after the operation was terrifying at first – painful – and I did avoid it as much as possible. I think it suited Stefano too, he wasn't particularly highly sexed and I was to find out why soon. Emotionally, I'd say I was still seven and was to stay seven until I confronted and dealt with my abuse many, many years later. I finally had a 'grown-up' female body and I was determined it was going to have all the fun it should have had between fourteen and my mid-twenties. All my friends were ten to fifteen years younger than me and I wanted to party with them. While most of my contemporaries had moved on to a more settled existence I had no employer, husband or family to worry about and

I pushed myself to the limit in socialising. I didn't seem to have an 'off' button.

I had Stefano – I would have almost described us as 'settled' – but the relationship was tempestuous and we both were doing drugs.

It was really the same old story. If I switched off I might have to think – and to think meant confronting the lack of stability in my life and what caused that instability. If I had stopped to analyse my situation, I might have realised that my operation had taken me only halfway along the road to 'wholeness'. There were even deeper issues, issues I could not allow myself to confront. So I went straight back into party mode as soon as my body would let me and hit the club scene with a vengeance; had several christening parties to 'wet the baby's head'. My life fell back into the pattern of clubbing, drinking and occasionally working to make enough money for clothes and nights out. I did have a permanent flat at this stage, courtesy of the Council, so at least I had somewhere definite to put down my head.

I think one thing I have to make clear is that I constantly lived a dual existence in London at this stage, and a lot of the time I wasn't even wholly aware of it myself. There was Rebecca, the glamorous model and hair and make-up artist – a true Londoner apart from her accent. To all outward appearances, and certainly to my fashionable clientele, I was living a high-powered, happy life in my new body. (In Ireland I had disappeared off the radar, spoken of occasionally at some big launch where models and media might mingle. "Whatever happened to flaky Ross Tallon?") But in London a second Rebecca was coming into view, one I'm not very proud of, a Rebecca who had been born in Amsterdam in the male brothel, one who was fuelled initially by the natural highs dancing gave her and later artificially heightened or dumbed down by drugs and alcohol. This second Rebecca was to gain the upper-hand gradually over the next twelve or thirteen years. If you look at the music and dance scene in London then, it went from High-Energy driven by E to Rave and Acid driven by cocaine. The music and dance scene were always where I went to fill my head, my heart, my soul with music and motion, and with that scene in London at the time came drugs. The drugs released me from being me, released me from the pain of being (I still felt) an outcast in society. And of course drugs, as had alcohol, took a ferocious grip on me eventually and brought me to the edge of an abyss.

But initially it was all 'recreational' use – a huge part in Stefano's life and the circles we moved in – or that was the lie we told ourselves and believed.

Stefano was determined to show me how much he loved me and he asked me to marry him. I was thrilled and got carried away by the romance of it all – teenage behaviour again. We had to go to Amsterdam to be married as my birth cert had me registered as male and couldn't be changed in Ireland, so it had to be a same-sex marriage which wasn't available in these islands at that time. This did irritate me, but I was used to prejudice and complete lack of understanding by the 'official' world at this stage, so I just did my own thing. It was to be 1997 before Lydia Foy even took her High Court case in Dublin and battled until this year (2010) to have Irish law changed so that her birth certificate, which showed her gender as male, could be re registered as female.

My relationship with Stefano, my beautiful smouldering Latin American, quickly showed cracks. I was a married woman and I changed my name by deed poll again to Rebecca Antoinette Tallon Alvarez. It had a lovely ring. And I had a family of my own again. A little unit. Someone special to be with in the evenings. This all proved to be a romantic dream though and my name was to become the only lovely thing about our marriage. Stefano was, theoretically, a translator. He did seem to be well-educated and spoke six or seven languages. He did the odd bit of interpreting or he taught a few classes teaching English as a foreign language. But in general he was quite content to loll around and sponge off me, partying and doing E at the weekends. During the three years we were on-and-off together he was almost always wired on something or other.

Stefano became intensely possessive of me. Unless he had organised the night out he didn't want me going out. He wanted to settle down and was quite happy to sit in most nights drinking and watching TV or listening to music, smoking ganga to bring him down off his latest Ecstasy high. The problem was he expected me to settle too and although I was in my mid-thirties I wasn't ready for settling – my girl body had lost time to make up for. I still wasn't ready to do quiet time, thinking time. I suppose the fact that I wasn't happy to do this, spend this type of time with Stefano, should have indicated to me that he was not 'The One', that special person with whom I wanted to spend the rest of my life.

Stefano would see me getting ready to go out and there would be an almighty row and I'd storm out effing and blinding and maybe stay out with friends for two or three nights to give him a chance to cool down. I don't know much about Brazilian culture but I think a lot of it is quite patriarchal and macho. Stefano had his own issues: his mother had abandoned him and he had been reared by his grandmother. I think he was always afraid that I too would leave him. Like me Stefano was intensely needy and two needy people in a relationship means hard work. For whatever reason he couldn't bear the fact that I was not prepared to play 'wifey'. I'd want to go out. I had to have people around me all the time – a throwback to the days of being sexually abused if I was alone with someone. If I didn't go out and we stayed in together the night would always end in a row.

Stefano grew fond of hitting me and on honest reflection I think I might have almost goaded him into doing that. It was as if it was behaviour I could understand. I could cope with people dumping on me, it was all I expected. If he reacted to me needling him then in my twisted logic I was in charge, I was making him behave like this. He would call me every name under the sun – a freak, no good for anyone or anything – he'd say no-one else would have me. And I'd believe him. I thought he was showing me what I was really like inside. Sometimes I'd get mad and think 'No. No. *This is not right. I am better than this.*' Then I would throw him out because the flat was mine or I would get out myself.

One evening after a humdinger of an argument in which he had used his fists on me I packed a suitcase, and taking my passport I left for Heathrow airport. The first flight out of the UK I could get that night was one to Dusseldorf – and that's where I went. I had stayed in contact with people I met years before on the gay and transgender scene and I stayed in Dusseldorf for well over a month.

One night in one of the clubs I met a charming man; a German businessman. I thought initially he was the bouncer in the club and he kept sending drink over to me. He was actually the owner of the club and had several other clubs. Transgender women were treated like goddesses in Dusseldorf at the time – and when I saw the Dusseldorf regular women I wasn't surprised. I know it was the fashion at the time, but they all looked like a cross between Bonny Tyler and Rod Stewart, all stiff bleached-blonde hair and stone-washed denim – it didn't suit *anyone!*

This man, George, was completely smitten with me and we saw a lot of each other over those few weeks. George was very wealthy and he pampered me; he actually spent a fortune on me buying me labels, Prada Gucci et al – he just loved the way I dressed and moved and he treated me like a Queen, a far cry from the way my husband treated me. I told him my story and how the marriage I had hoped would bring me such comfort was already crashing about my ears.

George was totally infatuated with me and he begged me to stay in Dusseldorf, on whatever terms I wanted. He said he would back me in business, anything. He was offering me the world. But I couldn't do it. I really liked him and it might have worked but in hindsight I'd say what put me off was his normality, his solidity. Perhaps in an uncomplicated easy relationship where any man was looking after me, or helping me look after myself, I wouldn't feel in control and I would be forced to confront internal demons I was not yet ready for. I was determined no-one, no-one, would ever be 'in charge' of me again. If my thinking had been that lucid at the time, I could have saved myself years of grief – but I think we all have to hit the bottom of our personal pits before we can crawl back out.

I got on a plane bound for London and some friend had let Stefano know I was on the way. He was waiting for me at the airport, arms wide begging for forgiveness and we got back together. But it was always going to be a disaster; he was poison to me, we were poison for each other.

It got to the stage that, if I wanted a night out with the girls, in order to avoid a row or a beating I wouldn't say anything at home. Then in the late afternoon I'd ask did he want a coffee. He'd grunt agreement and I'd slip a sleeping tablet in his coffee and shortly after he drank it he would zonk out and I could merrily get ready and head out clubbing. Nine times out of ten, when I came home he would have semi-consciously moved into the bedroom to continue his sleep. I would throw myself down on the couch and drift off.

Stefano would be all apologies the next morning, not able to understand how tired he had been and assume that he had driven me from the bed with his snoring. Then he would pamper me for the day to make it up to me.

As I said, funnily enough, although Stefano was intensely possessive of me and hated me going out with 'the girls', he never seemed to mind if I was doing escort work or even stripping. He knew me and my monogamous nature and he believed me when I said these jobs were just that – jobs, with nothing of a sexual or emotional nature to them – and, of course, he also enjoyed the money it brought in. This is hard to say and I certainly would not have worded it like this back then but Stefano Alvarez was, to all intents and purposes, my pimp. From cruising the clubs he would make contacts and get me high-paid escort jobs. He would escort me there and back. That really hurts – seeing it now for what it was. It certainly didn't do my self-esteem any good.

Barring a few months of initial contentment I have to say that I basically endured my relationship with Stefano – I did feel at times that I was better than we were, but I didn't know how to end it for I truly didn't want to be on my own. This was my first real relationship since Sam in the early 1980s. I would have done anything to make any of my longer relationships last, like all of us do – looking for love and wanting a little happiness. My conscience told me that Stefano was bad for me, wrong for me, but I just shut the voice down. He had chosen me and chased me, I must be worth something, he was gorgeous.

I was intensely cantankerous at that time. I was still on hormone treatment and my consumption of illicit drugs was increasing. This, on top of alcohol and with my childhood background, all meant that I was like a nest of wasps or hornets waiting to be disturbed. Like someone whose outer layers of skin have been burned away and whose inner skin is sensitive to everything – light, heat, movement. I know I was difficult to live with – but Christ almighty, why do some people have to beat the living daylights out of other people? Why can't they just walk away? I don't know whether it's the art of survival or what, but I seemed to be able to survive all these episodes and still keep going. There must be a reason for this, I would tell myself. I nick named myself Becky Forty-Lives because by rights I should have been dead a hundred times over. I still had my faith in Our Lady and I would chat to her, ask for guidance, ask her to help me stop making bad choices for myself.

Looking back, I can really see how I behaved like a little girl in the 90s, wanting to be mollycoddled and spoiled, totally dependent emotionally on Stefano, wanting someone else to be responsible for my happiness. I had to cling onto someone, even if that someone was sailing to hell in a handbag. I could safely say that in the three years I was married to Stefano we probably spent more time apart than together.

I rarely came to Ireland during those years. I did come to Dublin briefly in May 1995 and did *Kenny Live*, sort of a relaunch of myself in the public eye. Stefano and I were in one of our separated phases at the time, phases that were shortly to become long-term and I thought I might stay in Ireland for a while but I couldn't. Ireland wasn't ready for me yet. People still seemed to think I was simply looking for attention and that I would come to regret what I'd done. Jesus, if I'd wanted attention there were easier, less drastic ways to do it. Any time I did come home over the decade of the 90s was for a flying visit, to do a photo-shoot with one of the papers or to make a TV appearance. Occasionally to visit Mum. I continued to maintain the illusion at home that I was a successful model/make-up artist in London. In Dublin I still felt I was 'the freak', Ireland's very own transsexual to be taken out and paraded, then sent back in my box in London. Do I sound bitter? Well, I was, certainly, back then. Amazingly, no-one ever went digging to verify anything I intimated, so whatever nonsense I spouted was taken as verbatim. Being brutally frank, I was fully aware that the vast bulk of Irish people didn't care one way or another about me. If I could sell advertising space for the papers or the media so be it – it was really irrelevant what claims I made. I always returned London after these visits vowing never to go back to Ireland.

I never fully got Stefano's background from him, what his family did or how they felt about him being away. He would avoid the subject of his past and I know his mother abandoning him was a huge thing for him. Apart from being my pimp – I'd love to be able to say 'business manager' but it's too nice a term for what he was – he also slept with other people, although he wasn't particularly pushed about having sex with me, and he never went to much bother covering his tracks. Stefano had absolutely no respect for me and any respect I'd had for myself was quickly beaten out of me. Our relationship was over five years on and off of volatility. A train-crash waiting to happen, or more accurately a train-crash that had stretched over those years.

One evening, sometime very near the end of our relationship, I was due to go out and was halfway across the city when I realised I had forgotten something and came back to the flat. I walked through the door and went straight to the bedroom to collect it. There I discovered Stefano dressed in my clothes. He nearly died and he started to cry, begging me not to tell anyone. In ways it was the first time I had seen any real vulnerability in him. Looking back maybe that's what attracted me at first. I recognised someone like me; scared and vulnerable.

I assured him that I wouldn't tell anyone, but then he just clammed up about it, refused to discuss it. Whether he was transvestite and got enjoyment from dressing as a woman or whether he had a buried desire to be a woman I will never know. There is a big LGTG network in Brazil, particularly in the bigger cities, but it is a Catholic country and any kind of sexual 'deviancy', was frowned upon by the establishments. Stefano had his own demons I'm sure. But he didn't share them with me. Our sex life, quiet to say the least, really died about this time and some evenings I would look at Stefano and wonder where it would all end.

The years between my op and the death of our relationship were fairly mundane, workaday – the work being more night than day. I worked when I could, Stefano took E, smoked spliffs, drank and disappeared whenever it suited him. I'd throw him out, take him back.

We avoided each other a lot of the time, both of us staying overnight with other friends. We broke up finally in 1995, so we were actually together quite a long time – by my standards anyway. Although even then we still did try the odd time to make up.

One night in 1996 I was out in Stringfellows in Long Acre down near Covent Garden with a group of friends and we wound up in a late-night drinker in Frith St, off Old Compton Street. These bars opened and closed all the time around the city and word would get out and the crowd move from one to the other. There was a huge gang in the place that night and you couldn't even lift a cigarette to your lips. I came up out of the bar into the narrow cobbled street for air. I was alone on the street and I lit a cigarette and stretched my arms up over my head, loosening all the kinks in my body. I was wearing a pair of black Josef latex skinny trousers, black stiletto peep-toe shoes and a black ostrich-feather bra.

"Fittt . . . nnne . . . esss," purred a male voice behind me. I turned and laughed. It was a young man standing in a doorway, smoking. He was nineteen and absolutely stunning. A Stan Collymore lookalike. I honestly don't think I had ever met anyone in my life who looked as handsome as Robert did on our first meeting. Over six foot of lean muscle, impeccably clean and well presented with a shaved head and a smile that would cause you to swoon. Divine. And he was funny and charming to boot. He was at the late-night drinker with friends too and he started to chat me up. We soon fell into kissing each other and God, I couldn't resist him. We went back to my place in Draycott Avenue in Kensington. Stefano hadn't been there for months, we were officially over but some of his stuff was still about the place. I don't think Rob noticed Stefano's possessions – we only had eyes for each other that night and we fell into bed together. Actually I don't think we made it to the bed that first time. It was an unbelieveable night of love-making. I still shiver slightly with pleasure thinking of it. Robert would become my next husband and quite probably the love of my life.

The morning after our first night together I was rushing around all sixes and sevens. My sister Lucy and my cousin Cathy were over in London and I was due to meet them. Aunty Sybil and my cousins, Mary and Joanne, were also over separately to visit Sybil's son and I was to hook up with them later in the day. I discovered years later that Lucy's and Cathy's visit was no accidental coincidence – the primary reason was that Aunty Maureen sent them. They were all worried about me. Maureen and Sybil never ever stopped loving me, no matter what I did. They wanted to see me, to make sure I was alright. They were very special, caring people and I am privileged to have had them in my life.

When I got the second phone call to say Aunty Sybil was coming, I remember being delighted but sarcastically moaning, "Typical! Ye don't come near me for years and then there is a rash of ye!"

Rob could see I was all afluster and said, "Why so nervous, darling?"

"Well, this is the first time I've seen them since I had my sex change," I said, then realised I'd got so caught up in the heat of the moment the night before that I hadn't told him about my op! It was a cardinal rule with me to be totally upfront with anyone I intended to sleep with.

"I didn't know," he said, a little grey.

"Oh God. Sorry, I just automatically thought you'd know." I had never broken my rule until that night.

The poor fella, but I didn't have a minute to think about it then and I rushed him out the door making sure he had my phone number but neglecting to take his.

I met Lucy and Cathy in Luigi Malone's in South Kensington.

Cathy wouldn't have seen me in person since I'd had my op and her first reaction was, "Lord! You've shaped your eyebrows!"

It's funny the little things that stick in your head. I had breasts, long hair and was totally feminised, yet it was my eyebrows Cathy commented on! I was full of having met Rob and bursting to tell someone but, as I was supposedly still with Stefano, I didn't want to say anything in front of the girls. Lucy tried to ask me about Stefano but I kept avoiding the subject. I think she saw the strain in me and she did fill up when she was leaving me. She hugged me and told me to look after myself and I raced off to meet Aunty Sybil, Mary and Joanne at South Kensington tube station. I took them back to my flat. They stayed a couple of hours and it was so lovely to have family from Ireland in my London home.

It was that evening after all my Irish visitors had gone and my pals gathered before I even got a chance to think again about the amazing guy I'd met the night before. I couldn't believe I had let him out the door without getting his phone number! I sat in for a week, every night staring at the phone, pining – Lisa, Fay or one or another of my pals would join me and we'd drink and I'd cry. I was convinced this was it, he was 'The One' and I'd let him walk out of my life! My pals would console me, tell me I'd be all right. Oh Lord! It was so teenager-ish it's unreal. At the weekend they convinced me I had to go out, I'd get over him; I'd sworn Stefano was for life too – they couldn't understand what the hoo-ha was about; they knew I didn't casually sleep with anyone but it had only been one night – "Get over yourself, Rebecca!". These were tough cookies – animal attraction they could get but instant love didn't do it for them!

As I was ready to leave the flat the phone rang and I picked it up shouting into it,

"I'm coming, I'm coming, I swear!"

"Awright," purred the other end. "It's Rob."

"Oh God . . . I thought you wouldn't ring . . . that I'd frightened you off . . . I thought I'd never hear from you again." I was babbling and I didn't care.

"Actually," he whispered, "*I* thought I'd never ring you again. But here I am." He was ringing from his mum's house and was keeping his voice down.

I apologised for not letting him know about being transgender and he accepted my apology.

"I don't care what you are or who you were," he said. "I can't get you out of my mind. You are just the epitome of fitness."

I was flattered, I knew I had a good body but for this handsome young man to compliment me in the vernacular of the time meant a lot.

He asked what I was doing that night.

"Well, I *was* going out . . ." I said.

"Can I come over?"

It was ten o'clock at night and he had to get in from Leyton in East London. I fretted over this.

"That's my problem. I'll get there," and he rang off.

I rang around and warned everyone to stay away from me for the night. When the doorbell rang later and I opened it he sort of slid around it and kissed me on the lips. OMG! That man could turn me on so fast. It was magical and Stefano faded like a bad memory. Rob stayed the weekend and I 'had a viewing', where all my pals dropped by to have a look at Rob and approve him. Stefano had been very good-looking and could be charming but everyone agreed that Rob was the hottest thing they had seen in a long time. The only criticism they had was that he wore flip-flops around the house. I loved them! His lovely long golden feet and perfectly shaped toes shown off in a flip-flop! That man had no physical flaws.

Unfortunately Stefano got wind of the fact that I had met a wonderful man and decided to pay us a visit. One night in the week after our first meeting Rob and I had been out late and came back to the flat. I had a huge sofa and we made love. Rob was lying beside me, his head on my chest. I stretched my neck and extended my head back, almost purring. I felt this ... presence and I opened my eyes and who was standing over us looking like thunder but Stefano. He immediately launched into a rant at Rob about me being a married woman and still his etcetera.

"Do you know she's a fucking prostitute?" he shouted.

"I'm not a prostitute – I'm an escort," I rejoined.

Rob was pulling his clothes on and looking from one

to the other of us bewildered, poor man. First he had to cope with me being transgender, now he was hearing that I was married and a prostitute. With Rob's help I succeeded in throwing Stefano out and Rob asked me to be totally honest with him about my past. I was, and he promised he would help me keep Stefano out of my life. It was a situation that was to resolve itself very shortly anyway.

14

Love and Marriage – Third Time Lucky

I was thirty-seven and Rob had just turned twenty when we started to live together. I didn't see any anomaly in this, feeling there would be no societal reaction to it if the tables were reversed and he was the older man to my young woman. As I've said, emotionally and psychologically I was still very much a teenager.

I will admit to feeling a little nervous meeting his mum. He brought me home very early on in the relationship to meet her and his brothers in Leyton in East London which, while it impressed me that he was serious, was also a little intimidating. Rob was the youngest child in a family of three sons and his mum, Triona, was an East End Londoner. Rob's Dad was from Barbados originally. Triona and he were separated by the time I came into her son's life but they were still on fairly good terms and the dad lived in the next street. However he spent a good deal of time away from

Leyton on business and he also stayed a lot with his girlfriend who lived in another part of the city.

Triona took to me immediately and we got on really well. She was a very open loving woman who didn't care who Robert went out with once he was happy. And we were happy, at least in the beginning. I think Triona thought that as I was a good deal older than Rob, I might settle him a little. He wasn't working at that time and she worried about him. She was afraid that he would quite happily waste away his life. I really admired the relationship Triona had with her boys and as usual it reminded me of the huge hole in my life without Ava. A hole I never mentioned to anyone. Every time I talked to a parent and saw their concern for their children. Every Father's Day, Mother's Day, birthdays, Christmas, Easter. All of those days, the days when society makes a hoo-hah about family, little darts would pierce my heart, to go along with the bloody knife wound there already.

Rob was a complete sports jock, and played many games - football, tennis, golf – anything involving a ball. If he had been Irish I'd imagine he would have played hurling or football at county level. He was in great physical shape because of sports and he really looked after his body. He was glorious, a fun-loving, easy-going, wonderful young man. We had a very full and happy sex life together and I thought at the time; *This is it, this is finally it. I've made it home with this beautiful boy.*

Rob spent most of his time with me in the flat. It was

a nice airy flat and I was happy enough with the money I made from a few private hairdressing clients. There was always someone who wanted a cut and colour – it wasn't the steadiest income in the world, but then I had never really been used to a steady income. If work dried up, I could claim benefits and although Rob wasn't working he wasn't as high-maintenance as Stefano had been. The flat would get on our nerves at times though – it was still full of reminders of Stefano.

Rob wasn't 100% comfortable with some of the more flamboyant of my trannie friends. We tended to socialise more with his friends and I would often drop him across London to his dad's house. His dad had gone away for several months, and Robert was living in his house, supposedly to look after it. I stayed over there the odd night and, although the house was a bit dilapidated, it had loads of potential. It was always a bit of a haul back into the city if I had an appointment the next day.

Finally I suggested that we leave the flat for a while and try living together in the house in Leyton – I thought we could make something of it. I had a good eye for décor and could see the possibilities presented by the house. He was surprised and delighted.

"My bit of class," he used to call me and I'd laugh – the beauty of having an Irish accent in England is that they can't pigeon-hole you.

I liked Leyton. It was settled, a suburban area with families in it. I thought I was ready for this type of life, particularly with Rob. So we made the move but it was to be one I'd regret. It was fine in the beginning but the reality of living in an old house and attempting to make it more habitable, while Robert sat back and either criticised or disagreed with what I was doing, was enough to put strain on even the soundest of relationships. Plus while his family and most of his friends accepted me, there were one or two who were very unpleasant to me. Prejudice is an ugly thing. I'd get mad with Rob when he would tell me to just ignore rude comments. I thought he should defend me. I had let the flat in Draycott Avenue go but I decided I was leaving and took a flat in High Street, Kensington. Rob followed me there after a few weeks but not as happily as he had done before.

Around this time I launched a new business venture. I could see that the late-night drinking bars in Soho (mostly illegal) were moneyspinners and I was in one of them one night when the guy who owned it, an Irishman, said he was pulling out and going back home.

"Do ye think I could rent this?" I asked.

"I bet you could," he said.

So Rob and I opened Becky Boo's in Soho, near Berwick Street Market. I was really popular in that area – myself and my pals ran riot in it most nights and I always loved the area. It was so full of life – night and day there was constant noise and clatter. There were always people about, traders slagging us late-night early-morning revellers heading for home as they got stuck into a day's work. We had a sign made for outside the bar and the double 'o' of 'Boo's' were filled in like eyes with big long eyelashes. The bar was actually opposite one of the strip joints I had danced in as a male stripper years before for Madame Bouffe. We sank whatever cash we could get our hands onto into it. The place took off like a rocket and I couldn't believe the money we were making. Out of a couple of hundred pounds' worth of wholesale drink we made thousands. I ran the bar and got more and more involved in it and it drove Rob mad, watching me flirt all night with everyone in sight. I started doing the place up – delusions of grandeur as per usual – it was an illegal back-street drinker but I was going on as if it were Stringfellows. I got more and more involved in it and our relationship started to teeter over into constant rows. Eventually Rob got pissed off and left me, going back to Leytonstone.

One night, or rather morning, in early 1997, Stefano stumbled into Becky Boo's as I was closing. He was in a bad way, both drunk and high as a kite on something. He was crying; pleading with me to take him back.

I might have been insane but I couldn't leave someone I had once loved wandering incoherently around Soho so I took him back to the flat in High Street and threw him into bed. I fell into the bed beside him very shortly after that, exhausted. I was dreading the conversation we would have to have when he came to.

As it happened I didn't have to have that conversation. Fate intervened and took care of the situation. Stefano's drug use had grown and grown through our marriage and when we split he lost any vague control he'd had on his habit. Friends told me that he was almost constantly high on E or crack cocaine.

When I woke in the late afternoon I thought Stefano must be gone as the place seemed so quiet. I shifted in the bed and felt something cold. I lifted my head and realised it was Stefano. But he was blue grey in the face and stone cold. He must have been dead for a number of hours.

I ran, hysterical, from the apartment and down the stairs, screaming at the top of my lungs with no thought to the fact that I hadn't a stitch of clothes on. I roused neighbours who contacted the emergency services and rang friends for me. Within half an hour I was back sitting in my own living room, a blanket draped around me, shaking as I drank a cup of hot sweet tea that someone handed me. The whole flat was cordoned off with the police tape you only ever expect to see on television.

Of course word had got out, and every gay and trannie within walking distance had landed at the apartment to add to the hysteria. The decibel level was unbelieveable. And to pour gravy on the whole dinner for them all, I was arrested because the death looked suspicious. It was the talk of Soho for a week.

"Stefano Alvarez is dead and Rebecca murdered him!"

Thankfully the autopsy showed that Stefano had ingested enough Ecstasy and crack-cocaine to kill a horse and I was released after twenty hours; his death being ruled an accidental overdose.

There was all sorts of confusion after his death. Apparently he had married again (without doing anything about annulling our union in Amsterdam) and it was to his new wife that the body was returned. I never even got to pay my last respects at his funeral. Although I was sorry he was dead I cannot pretend to have been sorry that he was out of my life.

Rob heard of Stefano's death and came back to see I was okay, we made up and started living together again. This time with a little distance between us.

My religion still meant a lot to me, despite what individual members of that church had done to me and also despite knowing that the establishment rejected me. I never felt that Mary or Jesus or even God had abandoned me. God had made me what I was so he couldn't reject me, and Mary and Jesus were always there, they must have been because I cannot otherwise explain why I'm still breathing. One day in a little Catholic Church in inner London I was sitting praying, lighting candles for loved ones, when the local priest started to chat to me. He was a lovely man, very gentle and a great listener. He knew me from coming in and out. I told him about Rob and myself and how much I wished we could be married in the eyes of God. He told me that although he couldn't marry us he could bless out union. I was so thrilled. I went home full of excitement and Rob was delighted too, anything to make me happy. We had our blessing and that meant so much to me.

Everything was all right for a while and we made another attempt to live in Leyton. But I found it so hard to sit still at night in suburbia. I'd get fed up and pick a row with Rob so I'd have an excuse to storm out and go in to Soho to meet my friend Holly, who had a flat in Walker's Court near to the Berwick Street Market. I loved Holly and Kay, my drag-queen friends. Holly was Irish and totally outrageous – her own special creation. She was like Boy George exaggerated to the nth degree. We frequented Madame JoJo's off the Old Compton Road or The Piano Bar in Oxendon St until five or six in the morning. We'd stumble out of there in tiny skirts or the shortest of shorts, skimpy tops and knee-high boots. Holly in particular had the most outrageous boots – they were platforms made by Buffalo and were like cement blocks on her feet!

We loved it, we were home, Soho was our playground and we were like teenage girls teasing the men coming into work with barrows and trollies, bread vans, milkmen, flower sellers – it was like something out of *Oliver* and totally different to the more Faganesque face the area wore at night. We'd ramble around chatting to everyone and anyone, day or night. I never felt vulnerable in Soho. The Spice Girls hit '2 Become 1' was the big song at that time and, as Holly was partial to a Union Jack waistcoat a la Ginger Spice. We'd get tarted up and go on the razz, belting out the song at the top of our longs. We had a blast togethe~~r~~ out on the prowl, looking for laughs. I'd smoke s crack cocaine – which was becoming more a the drug of choice as people moved away from Ecstasy, or I might snort coke and get a little high, drink, dance, flirt, gossip. Filling my head with noise, movement and people. I'd go back to Holly's to crash and in the middle of the night Rob would turn up and shout up from the street that he needed to see me.

"She's not here!" Holly would yell down.

"She is. I know she is," Rob would cry. "I saw her car around the corner!"

Eventually we'd have to let him in to avoid someone calling the police. We'd make up and everything would be okay for a few days.

Sometime in 1997, I got a call from a researcher on an Irish chat show and was invited over to do the show in Dublin. I cannot for the life of me remember what show it was. I don't think it was *Kenny Live*. I think the interviewer may have been Seán Moncrieff, although I know I met Pat Kenny in the green room after the show. Rob came on the show with me and I was wired that night. I must have pressed the 'fuck-it' button before I went on. I went on dressed like Pamela Anderson in the movie *Barbed Wire*, all black latex and sexy, my twenty-year-old husband in _____ into Louis Walsh in RTÉ earlier that night and I _____ him grinning at me and saying "Go for it, give _____ nd by God I did. I don't think I was ever as _____ hat night.

_____ three grand and the fanny, seven," I

Rob was like a rabbit caught in headlights; he had never been on television before and I was very conscious of his discomfort. When we were having drinks later, Pat Kenny approached me and handed me a slip of paper, "You might want to ring that later," he said. A woman had rung the televison station and told the researcher that she was my half-sister and would like to meet me. I didn't think much of it, I hadn't kept in contact with my father but Lucy did get the odd word about him. I assumed this woman was his daughter. I met up with some of my family after the TV show and introduced Rob to them all. I think everyone was smitten by him. He certainly looked good and had that English politeness which so appeals.

The next morning myself and Lucy rang the number Pat Kenny had given me and what a story unfolded.

On this lady's birth certificate my mum was named as her birth mother. The baby had been given up immediately for private adoption. The date of her birth – and my mother's pregnancy leading up to it coincided with the time myself and my brother had been brought to the institution in Dublin. It all clicked into place with a sickening clunk.

Mum had fallen pregnant five years after my father left her. I can imagine Granny's reaction to that in rural mid-1960s middle class society. Granny probably washed her hands of the whole affair. She wasn't a young woman and having to cope with the fall-out from that in a small community would have been just too much for her. She had already been left more or less rearing the three of us while Mum was working in Dublin. Another baby brought into the already broken family would have been the straw that broke the camel's back. So Michael and I had been sentenced to five years in that bloody institution while Mum went off to secretly deliver another child. I was so angry.

Mum rang me later that day and she started to give me hell about my appearance and "slapperish" behaviour on the televison show the night before. I saw red and let her have it. The cheek of her! Calling me names and telling me off when her behaviour had caused myself and my siblings so much grief. Because Mum didn't have just one baby outside of the three of us. Our half-sister also told us that almost two years after she was born Mum bore another child, this time a boy and for another man, and that baby too was given up for private adoption. Oh, how the mighty were fallen!

I was actually surprised at how angry I was and Rob was reeling from it all. I have since met both my half-sister who lived in Dublin and through her my half-brother who was living in Newry at the time. In fact my half-brother and his wife came over to stay with Rob and me in London, one weekend later that summer. Although we argued so much that weekend that the poor couple ran out of the place and I haven't seen them since. Their tale is not mine to tell, and I have forgiven my mother all her failings as she forgave me mine. Resentments carried will sour your life – you *have* to flush them from your system.

Mum had her own demons and it is she who has had to live with them and with the fallout her actions caused. It was a different era, where a lot of moral hypocrisy existed. Appearing to do right in the eyes of society and particularly in the priest-ridden society of Ireland was that mattered. Anything else was hidden away. But I will admit it is something I found difficult to come to terms with. However, out of it I discovered more family, half-nieces and nephews many of whom I am in touch with to this day, so every cloud has a silver lining.

Rob and I tried to carry on with our life together. We were constantly in each other's company and all was well for a while. But cracks started to appear in mid-1998. Rob seemed quite content, like Stefano before him, to live off my earnings. He never worked in all the time we were together, unless he helped out in Becky Boo's when it was on the go. Rob and I would get into arguments which ended in screaming matches and I'm ashamed to admit that I would often be the one who threw first punch. I had to be the boss, and if I wasn't getting my own way there was hell to pay.

Of course, eventually Rob hit me back and the whole evening would deteriorate along those lines. Then he would be so remorseful when he'd calm down – barring on the sports field, he was by nature a passive man and he would be so apologetic. Although I hated this type of behaviour, it was like I almost drew it on myself. I understood it. I had been there before and could handle it. But gradually it dawned on me that I couldn't live my life forever like this. I was forty years of age in 1998 and still behaving like a girl in her mid-teens, still waltzing from one car-crash romance to another.

As 1998 gave way to 1999, I vowed that I would make amends, that my forties would be my best decade yet. I would put all old and dead wood behind me and move on to a better style of life.

Rob and I broke up a couple of times from mid-1998 into early 1999 and we would drift back together again. We had had such an intense relationship that we missed each other dreadfully. But things were falling apart for me. I was becoming increasingly more dependent on crack cocaine. I had always been thin but I lost about two stone in weight over a nine-month period. Rob would fight with me over my drug use; he was still smoking, but he was so mad into his sports that he never touched anything else. But there was worse to come.

Some of my friend Tia's friends – who were soon to be my friends – were confirmed junkies and we usually bought what we needed off one of them. Tia would let them use her flat to inject themselves or smoke rocks and in return they would 'go shopping' for us. One afternoon back in her flat, we had sent one of them off to get us some crack to ease us off a long night. He disappeared. I can't remember what happened – he might have been picked up by the police as he was a known user and dealer. Our skin was crawling and we badly needed a hit. Another pal of Tia's was there, sprawled on the couch.

"Cool it, ladies," he said. "Here, smoke a little brown."

We were horrified. Heroin! We couldn't do heroin. Sure that would make us junkies! We still thought of ourselves as recreational users. He kept at us, advising us if we were going to smoke a lot of crack or snort a line than we'd better make sure to always have a "little brown to mellow down". We didn't take too much persuasion – the perverted logic of the addict – we hadn't got hooked on coke, had we? We wouldn't be mainlining the heroin so we'd be all right, wouldn't we? We would. I took one toke and almost choked. The guy showed me how to hold it in my lungs a little and I copied him. It was like a flood of warmth flowing upwards from my ankles and tingling through my body. Like the best post-orgasm feeling ever. And so was born another addiction. After that if I bought coke I always had a little twist of brown stashed to ease me into the twilight.

I returned to Dublin for a number of weeks in early 1999, some time after myself and Rob had split yet again, and this time when I came back to London I got a place in Westbourne Park Road. It was quite grotty but it didn't bother me. Rob came to visit me once or twice and he was shocked at how much my physical appearance had deteriorated in such a short period. Heroin and crack cocaine will ravage you once they take hold. He begged me to stop using. I begged him to give us another go and he sat on the couch and his eyes filled with tears.

"I love you, Rebecca. But I can't live with you, I don't think anyone could," he said.

And with that he left.

He did call once or twice again and we would have slept together when he came to see me but I wasn't the person I had been and we both knew it. I pushed him away. I would have destroyed him and I did him a favour.

I heard Rob married some years later and that he had children. I hope he is happy. Maybe if I had met him at another time in my life, perhaps when I had all my 'issues' dealt with, then we might have stood some chance. I certainly loved him and regard him still as the one person with whom I might have been able to build a good marriage.

15

A New Millennium

Shortly after Rob left me for the last time I suffered an appalling sexual assault in that Westbourne Park Road flat. I used to let different junkies, with whom I had become friendly, shoot up and chill out in my place. In return for this safe haven they would go out and get me whatever I needed.

Please don't try to rationalise any of this within your own world. This was addict thinking, addict behaviour and it bears little or no reality to anyone's day-to-day life. Addicts are not automatically bad or criminal in any way. Both crack and brown should be called 'more'. Because after that first hit, that's what an addict spends the rest of the addiction chasing – that glorious first ride and more, and more and more, and eventually the 'more' becomes 'never enough'.

One day one of the lads had gone out to get me a few rocks and he disappeared. I was in bits waiting for him, shaking, paranoid in my need for a hit. This other guy – who I didn't know very well – called looking for my absent runner. I was in bad shape and I knew this man always had stuff so I pleaded with him for a hit. My benefit money was due the next day and he knew he would be paid. He disappeared and returned about twenty minutes later.

He watched as I prepared the hit and said, "Now. You owe me."

He left the flat and came back with three other guys a few minutes later. They raped me. One by one. Then one of them pissed on me when the dealer took my car keys and laughed as he left.

"I reckon you've paid now," he said.

I didn't report it. I didn't see the point. But thank God I was still *compos mentis* enough to recognise I was in real trouble and I went looking for help. In London they say that when you start smoking crack you are giving the Devil a blowjob and he keeps coming back for more.

Again I must applaud British Social Services and the NHS. They are unbelievably civil and helpful when it comes to those of us who are classed as 'vulnerable'. They tried, they really tried with me, time after time; even when I let them and myself down by falling off the wagon again and again. They were still there to help me make myself whole again.

London created Rebecca. I was effectively born there and it also watched me almost destroy myself. Then in London's own peculiar way it brought Rebecca back from the brink and reunited me with myself, with Eamon and all he had been through, and together we made another, better, more rounded person.

But the journey to that Rebecca was still to be a long one. If I'd had any idea of how long and hard the road I was setting out on in 1999 was, I don't know that I would have signed up for that first methadone maintenance programme. I really thought I had hit rock bottom and could go no lower. I dropped out of circulation, staying in touch by phone with a few friends, determined to be a better person.

The drugs unit within Social Services got me on the methadone programme and put me in touch with a 'vulnerable persons' group who helped me out. They came visiting and found me a lovely place to live in West Hampstead. It was a beautiful little garden flat with a bay window. It was a first let and I was so thrilled to be in such a nice space that I determined this was it. I was really going to clean up my act. I was disgusted with myself being on a methadone programme. I had visions of me mumbling, muttering and cruising my way into middle age on this stuff.

So I determined to go cold turkey. I had the half-bottle of methadone in the kitchen if I couldn't stick withdrawal, but I can be very stubborn if I really, really want to do something. Sometimes my will-power can be a rod of steel. Cold turkey is horrendous and don't let anyone ever tell you any different. It felt like there were maggots crawling under my skin and my body temperature went from freezing to shivering and sweating. I'd have freezing cold baths then boiling hot ones. Anything, anything to ease that intense neuralgic shivery feeling all over my body. I felt everything a thousand million times more than it was and I really thought I was going insane at times. When I woke on day five I realised I felt a little better. I wanted a drink so I knew I must be on the mend. I decided to sleep a little more first, then when I woke again I got up and made myself some toast and I lay on the couch watching TV. The window was open slightly and I could hear traffic and people talking and laughing, the sun was peeping in through the curtains. I felt quite proud of myself. I had done it, kicked a drug habit. I thought.

Time for adventure, I said to myself.

I hadn't set my foot outside my new home's door and I had been there a week. I tarted myself up, still looking worryingly thin and fragile but a thousand times better than I had done a few weeks previously and set off down the road. It was a lovely summer's day and West Hampstead is so pretty, like a little hamlet that has a real village feel to it despite being so near Central London.

I spotted a pub at the end of the street and decided to have a drink there. There were a couple of older people inside enjoying a bit of a chinwag and I got chatting to them and told them I'd just moved in. They suggested I came back that night when they would all be gathering with friends for a few drinks, a laugh and a sing-song. I was delighted with myself. It all felt very homey and just what I needed to bring me back from the brink of a heroin/methadone habit.

I started to go there most evenings and I was soon

drinking heavily every night. But I wasn't touching it during the day so the alarm bells weren't ringing too loudly.

I must have been going to the pub for a month or six weeks when I was at the bar one karaoke night and the place was swinging. I had got to know the manager, Timmo, quite well and I said to him, "Look at the life in here! This could be like this every night. I'd be great in here – you should give me a job!"

"Well, I will," he said and he offered me a part-time job.

I loved this job at the start. Then Timmo made me Assistant Manger and that was fine – I was well able to cope with that too. Then the pub needed a cleaner and that job paid eighty quid a week so I said, "Don't hire one, sure I'll do the extra few hours in the morning." Bad move. I was crawling out of the bed at half eight in the morning with a bad hangover usually, so much so that the shower would actually hurt me. Then I'd have to go into the pub and face the detritus of a night's boozing, and the gents' loos in particular would make me gag. So I started to stick a glass under an optic a couple of times to ease me around the cleaning. And so my road to hell was set.

I had a fancy for the guy who came to cook at lunchtime, Jonty. He was gorgeous and I'd flirt with him but nothing ever came of it. However the flirting cheered me up and I was getting a bit of pep in my step again. The vodka, I thought, was helping ease me back to 'normal' life.

As December approached I was thinking of Ava a lot. She would have been nineteen, heading into her twentieth year, and I was ready for her to come looking for me. How I expected the poor girl to find me is beyond me. But I did start to talk about my daughter to Jonty and anyone else who would listen at that stage, telling them all about her and how we'd been separated. I built it all up in my head, how lovely it would be if she came now. I was Assistant Manager in a nice pub and had a lovely little flat in a nice area. I would have been quite happy for her to have seen me in those circumstances. I thought she would be very proud of me, not even thinking of the amount of alcohol I was putting through my system. I'd fantasise about her coming to live with me and maybe we'd open a business together. I always had to think ahead, to dream of better times, of happy times.

I had lost large patches of hair to alopecia earlier in the year and when it started to grow back in it was really soft and shiny. I had it cut up short, the Lady Di look, and people complimented me on how well I looked.

I had a few bob in my pocket so I came home to Ireland for a few days before Christmas and stayed with my cousin Mary, bringing presents for her and her kids. It was lovely to see them all. Aunty Sybil was ill at the time. She was very elderly but she was still as warm and loving as always – as Mary has always been too.

When I returned to West Hampstead I started to wonder would it be a good idea to try Ireland again – I could see a change in society there, it was definitely finally coming out of the 1950s and that might mean I would find it easier to be accepted as a person in my own right. Once I no longer felt like Ireland's 'very own transsexual' I thought it would be okay.

We were throwing a millennium party in the pub on New Years Eve 1999. We thought, as Central London had out-priced itself, we'd have a good crowd in. However, everyone obviously decided to have house parties because in the pub that night there was myself, Timmo, Jonty and about six punters. It was the saddest party I was ever at. I remember the count-down to the year 2000 – looking in the pub mirror and watching the clock tick up to midnight, wondering what the next decade, the next century would bring me. I wonder, if I'd seen what was in store for me, the pain and degradation I was to go through over the next seven years, would I have gone home that night and drunk not only the methadone that still sat in my cupboard but whatever anti-depressants and alcohol were in the house? Perhaps not; but this retrospective look at my life has shown me how I went through a slow-pressure-cooker depression from 1999 which had really simmered from the time my childhood ended at age seven. The descent that started in that year took me to the gates of hell and from those gates I was delivered.

I find it hard to put down accurately the detail of the next seven years of my life. I quite literally don't remember a lot of it. If I had access to hospital records both in Ireland and London, I might be able to piece together an account with some sort of coherency. Things I think happened in 2005 were actually things that happened two years earlier when I try to pinpoint dates, using music or movies or something that would have been going on in the news. It was a long surreal *Alice in Wonderland* episode, except I was an Alice maddened by the 'Drink Me' bottle and my 'Wonderland' was a strange hellish place populated for the most part by people who were as wretched if not more so than myself. The only way I can write it for you is in the fractured flashback way I remember it. All the worst memories are the only ones deeply etched on my mind, and I will not swear to any date being accurate.

The only things I do know about myself at that time are:

1) I never knowingly did sexual favours for money and

2) I never killed or hurt anyone except myself.

Both these things would have been so low on my personal list of 'How low can Rebecca go?' that I'm assuming I would have remembered either of them. But I cannot swear to these things *not* happening and that hurts. I cannot swear.

I stayed working in the pub until spring 2000 – maybe summer. I got to know all the neighbours as they sat out enjoying the sunshine. I made friends and we would go to each other's houses for dinner. I always managed to control my drinking – never getting too drunk around people and never showing myself up. That's my recollection anyway. I almost felt like a teenager again, a little job, nice pals and neighbours. The area was lovely and I did feel quite settled there, particularly considering I had just kicked a drug habit. I had removed myself from the places I would frequent when I was doing drugs and I had created this little bubble of safety for myself.

I had always travelled to my addictions. Soho was my hellish playground, and around there were all my little dens of iniquity, my comfort zones where Rebecca the Addict could be Rebecca the Addict. For most of the time I tried to live a good bit away from Soho, unless I was totally bombed and crashing with someone. Ironically, when I finally went into recovery I was actually housed in Soho!

But in early 2000 I was busy ensuring that alcohol was my new addiction and it had no problem travelling to me. It got to a stage in my little West Hampstead flat where I couldn't get out of bed without a drink. But I still felt in control. I remember thinking, '*This isn't too bad, I can actually do this*' – be anaesthetized enough with booze, yet not so drunk that I couldn't function. If I didn't get too pissed and head for Soho to do crack cocaine, I thought I could toddle along quite merrily. But of course I lapsed on a regular basis.

Gabriel popped up regularly over the next few years. I became quite dependent on him for company when he was about and he would come to clubs and pubs with me and then disappear for a few days. Then when he'd turn up again I would be unsure if I'd had a row with him and chased him off. I couldn't trust anything. My memory was shot, my thinking too. I felt Gabriel was the only part of my more respectable 'upmarket club' life that had survived my sinking into alcoholism. Perhaps that was the reason I clung to him when he appeared. He seemed to have a remarkable intuition as to when I had money. God knows I had little enough of it. I couldn't wield a pair of scissors so was completely reliant on whatever little jobs I could get and when I couldn't get them I'd have my disability benefit.

My intentions not to get so drunk that I would end up in Soho never lasted long. I'd get fed up, get hammered and tarted up and land in Soho looking for Holly.

"C'mon, I need a few rocks!" was my battle cry, and off we'd go, Holly in all her regalia. She was one of the best drag-queens I have ever seen – her own style completely.

Holly's flat was at the top of a house, under which all the flats belonged to or were run as 'working-girls' flats'. These girls and all their entourage – the 'maids' (women who would see the punter in, check availability and handle laundry), the flat owners who called regularly for rent, the drug-pushers and shoplifters arriving with stuff for sale and the various hangers-on that seemed to congregate around – created a real buzz of activity. These working-girls had to turn about a thousand quid a day. The maid was paid £120 a day, the rent on the flat was anything up to £500 – daily. This wasn't high-class stuff – this was a string of men from early afternoon until the small hours of the morning at £20-£30 for ten or fifteen minutes. How can anyone deal with hundreds of men a week coming through like a conveyor belt and not drink or do drugs to block out the humiliation? But this is a business that feeds a whole plethora of people: the women themselves, their kids, their partners, their maids and the maids' families, the shoplifters and their families, the pushers, pimps and the junkies. A whole industry in one house in Soho.

The girls got to know us going in and out and I became really friendly with one of them – Sammi; I even did a stint as her maid. Sammi had two beautiful little boys and I learned years later that they ended up in care; and Sammi in and out of Holloway to do time for crimes committed to feed her habit. Sammi was still a lovely, young woman, a girl at the stage I knew her, but I could see her fate as I'm sure she could.

"Awright, darlin', lookin' for a model? Let's see if Sammi's free, darlin'. Just one minute now." That was my role: 'Look okay and show the way'. The cash I earned working for Sammi was easy for what it entailed and I could easily fit it in around my (at this stage diminishing) shifts in West Hampstead. Rocks of crack weren't cheap, not on top of a bottle of vodka a day. Again a dual existence – one that was getting harder and harder to maintain. I stopped working in the pub and let 'friends' stay in my flat in West Hampstead – which I then lost because the two who took it on thrashed it.

I came home for a short visit in August 2000 and there was a bit of a kerfuffle in my cousin Mary's house. I had gone to Club Anabel in the Burlington with friends and I got very drunk. A young couple picked a row with me outside afterwards. The man actually grabbed me by the hair and the girl was screeching at me, I don't know why – maybe I made some smart comment. I reached out to defend myself and scratched her on the arm. The bouncers intervened and the girl wanted me charged, despite witnesses saying that it was they who had started the dispute. She shrieked that she wanted to be taken to hospital to be checked over as I had scratched her and drawn blood and she was quite sure I had AIDS. I thought she was quite simply out of her head on something and just left it. However next morning two Special Branch men arrived at the house to question me. A young man had been murdered in the club that night and they wanted to see if I knew anything about it!

Of course I didn't – my incident had been unrelated. I was horrified and Mary more so. She had young children and because of an incident I had been involved in, innocently, there were policemen calling to the door early on a Sunday morning. Mary told me it wasn't on and asked me to leave. That was the beginning of the end really for me with family. Mary and her family had always been there for me and in fact even later on did help me when they could and are now very much part of my life again.

I went back to London, rented a little flat and as 2000 segued into 2001 my life continued to deteriorate. But I must have still managed to look respectable some days because in early 2001 the Abbey National granted me a loan of £5,000! I'd had an account there ever since I arrived in London in the late 80s and there always had been activity on the account. This was not planned – I was quite literally passing the building, wondered at my chances, popped in and applied for the loan of a cheeky £5,000 and amazingly I got it!

I thought this was great and went on a spending spree, treating myself very well because 'I deserved it'. I never, ever got over the shopping bug and my main addiction was and is shoes.

Aunt Sybil died and I came home for the funeral. I might have looked well in my Abbey National gear but my drinking was out of control and I only barely held it together. Mary and Andrea, my ex-wife, had stayed close friends and Andrea came to the funeral. We actually sat quite civilly together in the funeral car and greeted each other. I can still see people's eyes darting between the pair of us – wondering at the fact that we had once been married and produced a child together. I hadn't seen Andrea for fifteen or sixteen years and, although I was bursting to ask for news of Ava, I didn't. I would have asked Mary over the years but she was always very loyal to Andrea, and would say Ava was well but never gave me any more information – this was the way Andrea wanted it.

In fact I thought the whole civility of the funeral and the general acceptance of me indicated that I might pay a visit to Granard.

Two friends of mine came down with me and we had a great weekend. I hadn't been to Granard for years and people there would never have seen my full transformation to Rebecca. After the initial curiosity, it was lovely to have that feeling of acceptance – that feeling of home, I suppose. We stayed over Kitty Drake's Gift Shop – Kitty ran a bed and breakfast there and was always really good to me. The lads went back to Dublin on the Monday and I stayed on.

People kept coming to me and telling me what a brilliant cutter I had been: "Man or woman, ye gave the best cut in Longford!" They'd talk about Scruples, the salon I'd had there in the early 80s and about Ava. Women asked me to come to their homes and cut their hair before I went back to London. So it all started to feel very comfortable and my mind started to tick. I still had some of the Abbey National loan left (which I did eventually pay back!). I rang one of my friends who had been down with me for the weekend and he agreed to help me out with a few bob. And so my next salon in Ireland – Rebecca's on Main Street, Granard, opened.

16

No Place to Call Home

Foot and mouth disease had a grip on Ireland when I opened Rebecca's and, being in a rural community, I saw the full effect of it on trade. In fact, people thought I was mad trying to set up a business just then. All the businesses and houses had disinfectant mats outside the doors and people were trying to keep foot movement as contained as practicable.

I do remember feeling very much part of the community as I did up the little shop. All it needed were a few hand-basins and mirrors and a new floor. I had a steady clientele very quickly. I was a great hairdresser (they can't all have been wrong!) and I liked people, loved chatting to them. I was in my forties and I wondered; would this be it? Was I ready to settle in a little rented cottage out in Ballykilchreest with a battered little car to run around in? I felt safe all right – but it wasn't what I was used to, although I did try to make it what I could become used to. So much so that I even employed two juniors, Leonie, the daughter of my good friend Libby, and Leonie's cousin, Tracey. Libby had just lost her lovely son Graham in a car-crash and we'd sit for ages in the back of the salon, smoking and talking about him. I hadn't seen Graham since he was a small child but he had been the loveliest little fella then. He used to come into Scruples with Libby and he'd chat away to everyone, asking all the women what they were having done to their hair. He was blonde, cherubic and a real little old man, and now he was gone, robbed of life in his early twenties. Libby and I would cry for her loss and then we'd talk about Ava and I would look at Libby and we would cry for my loss back then. Because at times that's what it felt like. A death.

I did find it difficult being back in Granard from the point of view of memories. I seemed to see both Eamon and Ava everywhere. I still hadn't reconciled myself completely with the boy child I had theoretically been and I also started to obsess about Ava. I became determined that she should know me. If only she knew me, I'd think, she would see I wasn't a bad person. Of course along with this I was still drinking very, very heavily. I'd have one or two before I left the house in the morning to steady my hand. That would do me until Pettit's, the little local convenience store, opened and I could run across and get a bottle at which I would tipple all day.

I was never out of control. I never nicked anyone with the scissors or even gave them a Bad Hair Day.

Business was booming – if I had been incapable of cutting hair, I imagine the customers would have let me know. However, my sister Lucy worked in an office across the road from the salon and one day she dropped in and suggested I look at my alcohol consumption. Of course I lost the rag with her and we had a big row so she kept quiet about it after that. What could she do? I was supposedly an adult.

My forty-third birthday was looming and, because I hadn't celebrated a birthday with family in years, Lucy made these really clever invitations to people asking them to the third anniversary of Rebecca's fortieth birthday. My brother Michael, whom I hadn't seen in years and who actually had never met me as Rebecca, was coming down from Dublin for the party. I got all excited and invited all my pals, including the remaining members of the Stokes family who still lived about the town.

We held the get-together in Hourican's, the biggest local pub, and I spent ages getting ready. My hair was in a lovely sleek bob at the time but I put these extensions in and had a huge head of swirly curls. My cousins were all coming from Dublin and everything. Michael arrived and he had been drinking; he came over to me and told me how he hadn't been able to meet me unless he was drunk.

"I can't accept you the way you are," he said. "I'm sorry and I'm not proud of it. But I can't. But I want you to know. I love you. I loved Eamon and will always love him."

I found this hard. But it was just another thing to

bear. I'd borne so much at this stage it didn't seem another huge burden. I supposed at least he was being truthful.

But I did go to Lucy's house the following day. Still drunk, of course. I had stopped doing hangovers at that stage – I just never gave my system that option – I eliminated that part of the process. Michael was lying on the sofa, asleep. Lucy wouldn't let me see him because she knew I'd cause a row. So she got it too. I shouted the place down and left without seeing Michael but with him being in no doubt as to how I felt about him. I didn't mean it – all the hateful, hurtful things I said – but it was the easiest way out for both of us, me rejecting his half-hearted attempt at seeing me. I had loved seeing all the family at the party but Michael's reluctant appearance did sting. It more than stung – but stinging was all I'd admit to.

I started to party at the weekends in the Greville Arms and the pubs and even secured one or two dates with local lads for myself but they didn't work out. It's an awful pity I couldn't have done those few months in Granard in some state of sobriety. I might even have made a proper go of the business. But shit just kept on coming in my life.

One Saturday morning I was rushing into work quite late for my first appointment and Lucy rang me saying I had to come up immediately to her house. I told her I couldn't. I had Lena Stokes in at ten for a cut.

"Tell Lena I said it's urgent – she'll understand."

Lucy wasn't normally given to dramatics so I did as

she asked and drove to her house. I went around the back and in the kitchen door and there was a woman and little girl in the kitchen with Lucy.

I greeted them all and I said, "Lucy, what is it? It's Saturday, my busiest day, is there something wrong?"

"Rebecca, this is Lucy and her daughter Bonnie." Lucy was a bit pale.

"God! Two Lucys, isn't that unusual?" I put my hand out to the woman.

"Lucy is our half-sister," my full sister Lucy informed me.

I nearly fell out of my standing. My father had met someone else after all and this woman and her brother were his children. So I had more family. There were seven of us all told. The three of us, these two by our father with someone else and the two people who had come to light in 1997 that our mother had given up for adoption at birth. These people all had children so I had a squad of half-nieces and nephews. I could see my father and indeed our own Lucy in this Lucy. Bonnie was a pretty little child and she too reminded me of my little Ava as she had been years before, petite and delicate-looking. I had to rush back to my clients but we arranged to meet for lunch later. I went back to the salon and was shaking with the shock of it all. I told Lena and we just marvelled that things could still be happening in my life. Why on earth did strange events, things that normally only happen once in a lifetime to others, seem to follow me around? Did I have some big invisible sign on me saying *'Trouble, come and find me!'*?

I joined them later in the Greville Arms. There were the two Lucys, Bonnie and my half-brother Humphrey. We sat and chatted and then they had to return to Drogheda where they lived. New Lucy invited us to a family function in Drogheda in a fortnight's time and of course I agreed. Time for more adventure for Miss Rebecca and more family of course. I did go and I spent a good bit of time over the next few months travelling up and down to Drogheda getting to know Lucy and Humphrey and their friends and family.

In November 2001, I decided I wanted to go to Dublin to do some Christmas shopping for all my family, old and new. I've always been a sucker for Christmas and all the other special days that are marked by family, or at least marketed as such. I had plenty of cash and the salon was booked out from the middle of the following week until Christmas week so this was to be my last break before Christmas. My car was out of action so I got a lift up with this guy in a truck. We drank a bottle of vodka in the cab on the way up, laughing and flirting. I looked a million dollars and felt great – perhaps the last time for a long time I was to feel or look good, me to whom appearance had always been so important. I was wearing a beige suede trouser suit, a cream blouse and a pair of expensive cream leather stiletto boots – I loved them.

The boots are important – because when the truck driver dropped me at the top of Dame Street and I was getting out of the high cab, my foot slipped, the heel on one boot snapped and I was left with one leg half in the cab and the other heel-less boot hit the ground with a ferocious wallop. A sharp pain ricocheted up my leg and into my brain and I screamed. The truck driver nearly died but I insisted he went on, terrified he'd get done for drinking and driving. I hobbled to the nearest pub and ordered a treble Vodka and Red Bull. The woman behind the bar was killed trying to persuade me to go to hospital but I was having none of it. Three treble vodkas and – "I'll be grand" – I could feel no pain.

I left there and went on to The George and three days later I was still drinking. I have no idea of where I stayed, who I was with or how they put up with me. I had no Christmas shopping done and the foot would really not take any more no's for an answer. Somebody brought me to James Street Hospital and they had to cut the boot off my foot. I must've slept in the bloody things. Two of the bones in the foot were broken and I needed surgery to have pins put in. This was the Tuesday and I was due back to the salon in Granard on the Wednesday. I had lost my mobile phone. A loss that was to become a recurring motif over the next six years of my life. My life was in my handbag – the most important possessions I had (often the only ones I had), purse, phone and make-up were always in it – and I was constantly losing both bag and all its contents. I was kept in St James for almost a week, not knowing if I would ever get the full power of my foot back. Of course, once the effects of the anaesthetic wore off, I started to get alcohol withdrawal and persuaded friends to bring me in vodka. I was still tanked up and I intended to stay that way. I couldn't do cold turkey – not in hospital.

Granard in the meantime had been informed of my accident and all and sundry down there were totally pissed off with me. I had just pushed the neglectful button too far. I had to return to Granard for a few weeks but the reception there this time was very frosty. I had let a lot of customers down and was incapable of running the salon. I paid rent on it for a few weeks but eventually had to let it go. I knew it would be well into January before I would be able to run it properly again and, as January is a dead month in hairdressing, I would be starting out with a negative income. Tail between my legs, I had to let it go. I was too ashamed to hang around Granard so I left for Dublin. I stayed in grotty bed and breakfasts on the Northside of the inner city and drank my way into Christmas week.

On the 23rd of December 2001, the day after Ava's 21st birthday, I caught the last train to Edgeworthstown, in bits yet again, reasoning that Lucy would let me in. No matter what, she was still my sister and still loved me and sure how could anyone turn me, on crutches, away for Christmas. There were no taxis when I got into the railway station so I thumbed a lift and was left at the top of the town at the spot where the Corner House had been. The town was incredibly quiet and I didn't run into one person as I limped along the main road out towards Lucy's house on my crutches with a small knapsack on my back. It was a very cold and icy night and I was terrified I would fall and freeze to death before someone found me. I made it eventually to Lucy's door. It must have been about 10.30p.m.

As she opened the door, her husband Dick came out into the hall and jabbing his finger at me he said – "No – he's not coming into this house and disrupting our Christmas!"

I never got on with the man and we were only ever barely civil to each other, but this really shocked me.

Poor Lucy had to send me on my way. I was devastated. I knew Lucy was having 'marital difficulties' at that time but I really hadn't expected that. Their marriage broke up not long after this incident.

I had pushed Lucy once too often and I knew better than to try again. I didn't even try to get a bed and breakfast at that stage – I was truly afraid I'd be refused, apart from anything else. One of the pubs in the town was still open and I stayed there until closing time – drinking and licking my wounds. Then I hitched back to Edgesworthstown, getting there about three in the morning. I sat freezing on a bench by the railway station until the first train to Dublin left on Christmas Eve. I was gone beyond feeling at that stage. I was in a complete daze.

I found a hostel down around Talbot Street that was £8 a night and had a place where I could securely lock away my bags. I made friends with other people there, almost all in the same boat as myself – most of us suffering from alcoholism and other addictions. Our common theme was incredible loneliness. We managed to have plenty to drink on Christmas Day anyway. Vodka and a Mars Bar – that was my Christmas dinner in 2001. I got up on St Stephen's Day and I hit the drink again – actually there was no 'again' – I'd drink, pass out, wake up, drink, pass-out and so on. I could be very cantankerous when drunk and I knew some of the people in the hostel wanted me out and I remember being really afraid. Jesus, if they weren't prepared to keep me in this dive, where in the name of God would I go? I was the most incredible mess – in every way. Where did it all go wrong? I was moaning, blaming the world – everything was great, lovely little business, plenty of family and now it was all gone. It was not my fault, none of it. I could not blame my drinking, because if I did then I would be responsible and if I was responsible then I would have to stop drinking to stop the chaos.

I met a Dutch guy in a pub in Talbot Street who took a fierce shine to me – or seemed to and kept buying me drink. I would have gone off with Osama Bin Laden if he had kept my tank full at that stage. Dutch was all over me and begged me to come to Amsterdam with him for the New Year.

"Of course I'll go – sure I know Amsterdam well." I would have gone to Argentina, Sierra Leone – anywhere. He also promised to pay for my boat fare home.

The next thing I really recollect with any clarity is coming to in Amsterdam as 2002 was rung in and people shouting "Happy New Year!".

I looked up at this man and said, "Where am I and who are you?'

He told me his name – "Dutch" – and it was vaguely familiar.

When I thought about it, I recollected being on a boat. It had been quite luxurious and I remembered a big fuss because I had no passport and the staff on the ship and Dutch trying to sort some sot of emergency papers for me – but beyond that I can't say, just absolutely no idea – and I don't know that I do want to remember. It all seems a little sinister at this point in looking back. Another guy told me later that I'd been used as a drug mule – not carrying anything – but that the state of me, drunk, painfully wretched-looking and pitiful in the plaster of Paris, crutches et al was enough to divert attention away from my Dutch friend's incoming cargo.

Dutch had told me he would send me back to Dublin but he refused at that stage – I had done what he needed me to do. His friends got together cash to get me there – maybe more to get rid of me because I was a liability by then.

When I got back to Dublin I went back to the hostel and then spread myself out among friends, half-friends and vague acquaintances, cadging a bed here, a shower there. I was homeless, a vagabond. The only step I had left to take was sleeping on the streets and drinking on a permanent basis with the winos. This was fucking scary and it had got to the stage that I was even semi-sober a lot of the time. I couldn't block out any of the pain, the pain of being the raped child, the rejected body, the parent who has lost her child. At that stage I was only drinking to prevent the horror of sobering up.

A man put me up one night and he said he would give me a bed, shower and I could even drink in his place – in fact he even bought the drink for me but only if I would agree to try the Cuan Mhuire six-week addiction therapy course in Athy. I had nothing left to lose and I agreed. At least I knew where my bed would be for the next month.

We got the train down and I went into Cuan Mhuire absolutely locked out of my head. I know Cuan Mhuire has saved people's lives and that Sister Consilio is a really wonderful woman, but the course wasn't a success for me. I think maybe because I didn't consciously make the decision to go in myself or maybe the fact that I had still further to fall meant that it wasn't yet time for me. I did five weeks of the six – drinking at times in the bushes with some of my co-alcoholics and I contacted family and let them know I was at least trying.

During this time a woman, Maria, started to visit me, I'm not sure how, perhaps through some voluntary charitable group. Maria came to believe in me and she was prepared to put me up and help me out when I was discharged. She was a real Good Samaritan and I stayed in her sister's house – the sister had a spare room. Unfortunately there was drink available in the house and the temptation was too much for me and within a week I started to drink again. Maria was quite prepared to help set me up in a salon and everything. I had obviously told her about my failed salon in Granard. To be honest, I have no real recollection of agreeing to any of this – I'm sure I did but my mind was completely blown at this stage. In any case I pulled out of the whole deal.

I did have a little money left and I made my way back to Dublin where I somehow cadged together enough cash in May 2002 to take the boat to England.

Flash forward to London. Fuck Granard. Fuck Ireland. Soho would welcome me home; Soho loved me.

17

Down and Out . . . and Up and Down

When I got back to London I stayed in Islington with my friend Jason and I spent a lot of time with Jodie and Charlene, two other transsexuals. We were drinking very heavily and I started doing rocks – crack cocaine – regularly. Then I got onto heroin again, smoking it to come down off the crack. I was back to square one – never having got too far beyond it. I spent every night out, down about the West End clubbing – in all the gay clubs only at this stage. I was too shattered-looking to get into any of the upmarket straight clubs and at some subliminal level I was aware of this and avoided them. The funny thing is, in all my worst years a lot of the people I would have known from these clubs never saw the wretch I became. I had somehow still managed to keep the two lives separate.

I really think that this was truly when the 'fuck it' button was hit. I felt I had been given my second chance in Ireland, my little business in Granard and my chances with friends and family and I had fucked it up. There was no hope for me – but I wasn't going to go out quietly – no, Rebecca was going to burn out like a flare – bright and glarey until the last minute. I had nothing, absolutely nothing, left to lose. The types of decisions that other people take months to make I made in five minutes. I couldn't see beyond the end of the next drink or hit anyway and if I could it was to think, '*London's where I'm gonna die – at least they'll give me a pauper's grave.*'

I got back on benefits and moved down into Soho. Soho – once my playground was now the hell-hole I crawled into to die. I felt at least I wasn't alone there. I wasn't drinking or doing crack on my own – there was a little ghetto of about ten of us and our behaviour was, at best, puerile; at worst, the cat fighting and attempted physical fighting was ludicrous. The bitching was incredible as each of us addicts tried to look after our personal habit's needs. These, mostly girls, were kids who for the larger part had grown up in deprived backgrounds in East London – they had little or no education and came from homes that had been riddled by drink, drugs and violence for generations. Most of them had been on the streets and had worked at prostitution from a very young age and most of that little group are either dead or in prison now. Poor kids, they truly never had a chance. And there I was, in the middle of them all – holding my own – but only barely.

I did try to get a job as a 'maid' again in the

'working–girls' flats' but my drinking and general behaviour had got so bad, and I looked so wretched, that even they wouldn't employ me. How bad was that? The prostitutes in the rooms in Soho wouldn't employ me!

At this stage I was avoiding everything except drink and drugs. I knew the inside of every Accident & Emergency in London. I was taken into police cells for my own protection and when they let me out I hobbled the streets of Soho, a screeching banshee, a wailing harpy. I didn't give a fuck. Or did I? What in the name of God kept me going, kept me putting one foot in front of the other?

On more than one occasion I was taken into respite in hospital to be treated for malnourishment. The medics would dry me out over a couple of days (never fully – there was still always someone willing to get me drink or drugs for a cut), patch me up, strap up any broken or sprained limbs, clean me up and set me back outside the gates of the hospital. Where I would begin the whole self-destructive circle again. It got to the stage that some of the doctors in one hospital refused to treat me for anything other than a broken limb – I wasn't making any effort to rehabilitate myself and they felt it was a waste of resources. I remember standing outside a police station one morning and going back in to complain that the name of the particular station wasn't up outside the door. I hadn't the faintest idea what part of London I was in. My times of knowing who I was, or where I was, were very, very few and quickly blotted out with more booze, drugs – whatever pain relief was to hand. There was no pleasure in any of this, no pleasure in anything – none.

I can't really put a timeline on this period – I think it went on for almost two years but it may have been longer or shorter, may in fact be confused with incidents that actually happened years earlier or later. All I know is day segued into night, week followed week, month month and I was still fucking here, still on this fucking planet. A sad six-stone emaciated person, in a tiny miniskirt, high heels and a skimpy top – everyone's notion of a tramp with no lower to go. I would come to from blackout and start again and again, and again. I genuinely do not know what kept me alive.

Something might click in me and I'd go cold turkey for a couple of days. On one occasion I was really in a bad way coming off everything, and to cap it all I got a dose of shingles – they are incredibly painful and I quite literally could not move. I kept watching them growing around me and was terrified they would completely encircle my waist – I could hear Granny and Aunty Maureen chatting about them years before and saying: "You're all right unless they make the full circle. You die if they make the full circle."

A junkie friend of mine said I was insane – I'd have to go to hospital. But I begged him for some brown, just a little, then I could get clean in hospital. He actually half-carried me to the hospital and I was wailing like a banshee the whole way. We must have looked a right pair. The hospital wouldn't take me in that time – not unless I was clean. That's how bad I was. Another hospital did admit me and transferred me to their psychiatric clinic where I was offered a methadone programme. I chose cold turkey. I hadn't seen methadone working for anyone. People seemed to end up using both it and heroin.

I was, I think, probably more than a little mad at this stage – and what did I do? Why, went back to Dublin of course. I'd give Ireland another go. I'd be away from the worst of the drugs. Sure, there were no drugs in Ireland. That's the way my mind worked: I had never done serious drug use in Dublin so therefore for me it was a safe place.

This was early spring 2004 and I landed in The Front Lounge in Parliament Street all smiles and bones. Panti, Empress of Drag Queens, actually seemed pleased to see me, or maybe she was just an extremely talented actor. I met up with old friends and started to party and, as I was south of the river, I was on my reasonably best behaviour.

Within a week, a friend and I had hooked up with a couple of men from Belfast and we were invited up there for a weekend. We went with no hesitation and found that one of the men owned a huge villa of a place off the Shankill Road which was run as a Bed & Breakfast. This man had taken a fierce shine to my pal and I was thinking, *'This is great, I've landed on my feet with no strings.'*

My friend wanted me about initially for a bit of security, I think. The Belfast guy gave her plenty of money which she shared with me and we had a lovely place to stay in.

So what does Rebecca do while her pal is busy with new boyfriend? Rebecca wastes no time finding the nearest watering holes, and the working-men clubs on the Shankill didn't know what hit them. A Catholic transsexual woman – who was partial to rosary beads and Miraculous Medals. I was an instant success.

"Here she is, the only Catholic allowed to drink in here, the only brave one of the whole lot of them! Fuck Kevin Barry and all them, we've got Rebecca Tallon! What's yours, love? Triple vodka and Red Bull – put that on the bar for the wee lady!"

If I hadn't been so drunk all the time I might have either been nervous or laughed. The man who owned the Bed & Breakfast got a little nervous over my choice of drinking buddies and asked me to leave. He didn't completely throw me out on the street, however. A friend of his owned a little caravan park not too far off, and he let me stay there in one of his caravans. It was spring and still bloody freezing and there was only one other caravan occupied. The couple who were staying in it were friendly and they would bring me back my 'shopping' if they went to town – basically my vodka and fags. One night the woman took me outside of the caravan, insistent that I look at the lights of Scotland on the horizon. I laughed and I can still hear myself saying, "Sure I can't see anything. I'm blind drunk."

I fell out with them shortly after that. I cannot remember why but I take responsibility for whatever it was, so I had to leave the caravan park. But I realised that as I was in the North my benefits were transferable from London. So I presented myself to Social Services and told them I was homeless. They housed me up in the area of Belfast called the Holylands (because of the street names) and the street I was given a flat in was Magdala Street. It was a miracle, I decided. Our Lady was telling me to stop drinking and I decided that I should at least *try* to get dry. I found a support group and painfully started the process to an alcohol-free life. I think I did four or five meetings a day in the beginning and I got stronger every day.

I put on a little weight and started to look after my health and I actually succeeded in staying dry and clean for almost five months. I got really involved in the support group and in other voluntary activities, including helping out in a hospice. I even went away with some of the patients to Donegal for a respite weekend. I was reformed and delighted with myself. Because I was classed as disabled I was entitled to a car from Social Services. People give out about the Nanny State when they hear that. Why? I have to be either self-employed or treated as disabled because employers shy away from me, reject me – but am I a reject? No, not unless I let myself be. I have very often let myself be. But I had up to this always managed to crawl away and make myself fit again. I will always bear the social and cultural stigma of not fitting a narrow interpretation of what a person should or shouldn't be. My life had been a series of the highest of high highs and the very dregs of lows to this point – but there were further depths and heights to be plumbed.

I started to make little trips to Drogheda to see my half-sister and brother and to Dublin to see friends and even my mum! She finally accepted me back into her life. Since our bust-up in 1997, relationships had been very, very frosty – now, although we tiptoed around each other, at least she was talking to me.

I started to sort out my paperwork in the Republic of Ireland. I actually was awarded the first Irish passport in which a gender description was changed from 'male' to 'female'. I remember the civil servant who handed it to me congratulating me and shaking my hand. A red-letter day for me.

In July that year, I left Belfast to travel to Dublin. I wasn't comfortable being there for the Twelfth celebrations, the day the Orangemen of Ulster march with pipes and drums, all over Northern Ireland, to celebrate the victory of Protestant William of Orange over Catholic James II at the Battle of the Boyne, July 1690. Violence inevitably erupts so I had arranged to stay with family. They were all delighted I seemed to be getting myself together. I was driving the Volkswagon Golf that Social Services had given me. I thought I was going to land back in Dublin with a bang – 'Look at me, guys, I got it made!'

I did land with a bang, literally. I was involved in a head-on collision on the Newry-Dublin road. I have no idea how any of us survived it – myself and the two occupants of the other car. All I can remember is everything being knocked out of 'sync' and smelling something strange. Then the next thing I recall is a fireman was cutting me from the car. Later I discovered that my car and another had smacked into each other. The guy and his girlfriend had minor injuries and I had to be cut from the car. I was taken to hospital. Eleven stitches in my leg and a bruised and battered collarbone and ribcage. The funny, comical funny, thing was that when the cars collided the boot of my car exploded open with the impact and all my shoes – Rebecca Tallon stiletto specials – which I always threw loose into the boot, were spewed across the road. The boots and shoes were the first thing I saw when the firemen got me out of the car and despite the state I was in I wanted to collect them all together. My babies! I laughed weeks later – when I could see the funny side.

So I was back in Dublin, bandaged up and carless. The accident had made me nervous about travelling and I decided to maybe give Dublin another go. On an earlier trip to Dublin that year I had run into an old friend, Paul. Paul was living with a Brazilian guy who was about to be deported. These guys were crazy about each other and desperate to stay together. Paul contacted me and asked if I could help them out by marrying his Brazilian boyfriend in Newry. I was legally female in the UK, my passport showed me as female and my papers showed my gender reassignment. The lads told me they would give me the few bob I needed to kick-start a life in Dublin again for myself. I found that people were accepting me back in Dublin and started to wonder could I do it again. I moved in with Paul and his partner and things were looking okay. I was sober. If I was sober I could do anything – maybe I could go back hairdressing – nothing seemed impossible anymore.

I really thought I had my life back on the straight and narrow. I wasn't as lonely and it was certainly the longest period I had done sober since I started to drink seriously in the mid-90s. However, I couldn't go through with the marriage. I would be marrying someone I didn't know simply for money. Ultimately, my conscience was prickling about it and I knew I wouldn't feel good about myself – I was really on the road to recovery. I ran into Gerry Lynch, an old friend – actually the guy who had been with myself and Louis Walsh when Sam and I had the 'Easter Egg Fight' in the early 80s! Gerry was very involved still in the music and club scene in Dublin. I talked to him about my upcoming nuptials and he agreed with me that the marriage wasn't a good idea – he told me people were just beginning to trust and respect me again and he felt if I did this I would be letting myself down more than anything.

I pulled out of the marriage agreement and I wasn't the most popular person for it. I had to move out of the lads' place – but I'm glad to this day. I moved in with a friend of the lads, Mae, and shared a flat with her. Mae was delighted the wedding hadn't gone ahead because she too was cracked about this Brazilian man but hadn't been able to marry him because she was pre-op and therefore still legally male. Every cloud etc!

Mae worked for the LGBT rights office and I was involved with them on a voluntary basis. I wrote the odd article for a gay magazine and Gerry Lynch gave me a job working in the cloakroom in his club Yellow, so it was a little start. I started to organise a fashion show to be held there in Christmas week to raise money for the LGBT. I was back showing models how to walk – creating hair and make-up looks and organising clothes – the things I was good at. I was still painfully thin, maybe seven and a half stone, and would have looked rake-thin in a tight dress – sort of Victoria Beckham size. But I was proud of myself – I was 'mending'. Lucy even came to visit me mid-December 2004 and although I wasn't invited anywhere for Christmas it was a step up from being refused entry two years previously.

In my own little bubble of a world I was 'getting back into the fashion business' – I knew it was in a tiny way but it made me feel good and started to raise my hopes.

The fashion show went really well and Mae and I were pleased with the night. Mae was going home to Cork for Christmas. She bought me a darling little Westie pup, Dolly Sue, as a present – I was delighted. I spent Christmas 2004 with my little dog. Unfortunately, I was still very lonely and I also reintroduced the bottle of vodka. My drinking was slow at the start but it didn't take long for the negative addictive thinking to start. When Mae came back to Dublin we had a huge row, over very little, and she left the flat. I was drinking heavily at this stage and when I returned one evening it was to find she had sent friends in to clear out all her stuff and they also took Dolly Sue. I was heartbroken and was disgusted with myself. I had reverted to type and as I was drinking again I was getting the cold shoulder a lot of places I went.

I did have a few friends and one of them helped me get a little bedsit in Ballsbridge. I moved in and actually met Mum for lunch that day in the Horse and Hound Pub. She looked great, so sophisticated and well-dressed – I was really proud of her and thought I'd maybe get my act together this time. Unfortunately this little bedsit turned into a little hellhole for me. I kept drinking heavily and anyone with a bottle was welcome. I didn't keep the place too tidy and I was fast degenerating back into the mess I had been before Belfast. I would call over to my cousin Mary's house and eventually even she, the most patient of my family to date, had to ask me to stop calling when I was drinking.

I'd try to stop. I'd go to a support group meeting or two. But it just wasn't working for me.

18

The Final Meltdown

Oh God. Even writing that chapter name – one would think that by now I had hit so many 'fuck-it' buttons and 'this is it' stages that I would either be dead or reformed – but I had a little further to go.

We got word that our dad had died in England on March 18th 2005. I couldn't pretend to be upset. I had only ever met the man twice and had had no wish to meet him again. Lucy had kept in touch with him sporadically and she would let me know the odd time she heard anything about him. He appeared to have spent most of his later years in England. Another exile. There were uncles and cousins and family members – Dad's side of the family – who had really played very little role in my life (no fault of theirs – it was simply the way life and Irish law made it – in fairness, bloody universal law). They got in contact and said to come on over to the funeral.

Lucy was going to go and I said: "Look, I'll go too – may God forgive me, just to make sure he's dead."

Lucy said she'd see me there. She wouldn't travel with me because I was drinking and she told me so. We arranged to meet over at the funeral. I had long stopped taking offence at my family not wanting to be around me because of my drinking. It suited me and I recognised that they were the only ones left who cared enough to even try and stop me. I knew I had a problem but I had tried to do something about it and failed. Almost every day I would think about quitting, I knew everyone thought me a lost cause but I still entertained this mad hope that something was going to come along and make it easy for me just to stop. I stopped drinking every night I passed out. And started again as soon as I opened my eyes every morning. My foray at home hadn't been the success I had hoped. I succeeded in avoiding drugs but alcohol was still the main staple of my diet, drinking mainly in the flat but occasionally I would go out to local pubs and black out, not remember getting home but always managing to get there.

Mary helped me with the cash to get to the funeral and I did all my research, booked flights, checked trains and tubes, booked a Bed & Breakfast in Bayswater and set off for England yet again. I really did mean to go to the funeral, if only to meet his, and therefore my, extended family. The night before it I got myself all tarted up and went out and got 'rat-arsed' – for those of you without Hiberno-English, imagine a stupid rat chasing its own tail in the hope of achieving something – what? – the rat has no idea, but it appears to be enormously important; at least to the poor rat. So what happened? I wandered around Soho – mourning the dad I'd never known – telling all and sundry I was burying him – people buying me drinks to sympathise.

I met Vivian, one of the girls I used to do drugs with.

"Babe, babe, you look so great! Gel, you look fantastic – so classy!" she schmoozed – basically, 'Have you any money?'.

I sighed – home sweet home, no pretence necessary.

"Have you any rocks?" was my first question.

I don't remember the rest of the night – sympathy, booze, crack cocaine and smoking heroin. Eventually landed back by yet again another miracle to Bayswater and I lay down – and actually set the alarm! But slept through it and didn't wake up until 1p.m. – Dad in the dirt and feeling shit. Forget about everyone else, I had let myself down, proved myself as unreliable as the man who had fathered me. And it tasted bad in my mouth.

So what did I do – back down to the West End – *'mourning and weeping in this Valley of Tears'*, looking for pain relief as always.

And eventually (although in my fractured brain it was suddenly) days, weeks, months had gone by and I was still cruisin' with Vivian. I had left everything in my grotty Dublin bedsit – clothes, TV, stereo, electrical goods and I genuinely don't think I even noticed. I was back on benefits and picked up enough cash to feed whatever habit I decided to have.

Vivian lived with her mum and brothers and sisters in a big Council estate and I moved in with them. So I had a bed, or at least a roof over my head and Vivian's mum, and I got on. She was an alcoholic as well.

Everyone who lived in that place was on benefits and there were people doing heavy drugs in lots of the flats. These were four-bedroomed Council flats in a horrible building and the dealers never stopped coming. The doors never stopped going, morning and night, and people shrieking: "Who is it? Yeah. Right." Door open, money exchanged and deal done, door closed; until five minutes later when the whole process started again.

Vivian's mum and I would sit smoking and drinking in the kitchen talking about home. I had become even worse than the sad Paddy in County Kilburn I had sworn I would never become – lonelier and more broken. Vivian's mum got her money on a Tuesday and mine came on Friday so one or the other of us could always supply the vodka and the fags.

But Vivian's mum died a few weeks after I moved in and I can remember trying to get Vivian out the door to her funeral. The old-fashioned hearse, drawn in the traditional East End fashion by four black horses wearing black plumes, was waiting on the road for us. Vivian couldn't leave until she had shot up one more time.

This was in summer 2005 and I was doing drugs

regularly. With Vivian's mum gone, I noticed a change in Vivian and the others. They would tease me, torment me with drugs. I had been using heroin for the longest time yet and I knew I had to get off it – it was getting a terrible grip on me and it wouldn't be long before I'd have to go down and be a streetwalker. I couldn't bear the thought of it – it was just one step too far for me. I could never imagine any emotional attachment to a kerb-crawler and so would have to break my rule of only engaging in full consensual lovemaking with someone I cared about.

I remember one morning catching sight of myself in the long window of the room I slept in. It was intensely cold outside and condensation had formed inside (as it will if you stuff all window and door drafts). I genuinely was horrified by what I saw, a bag of bones covered by loose folds of sickly looking skin and it tipped me into reality for a brief time. I thought, *'Jeez, Rebecca – you've got awful skinny!'*

Then I noticed that these flippin' welts had started appearing on my face and when I checked they were all over me. I was still clued in enough to know I needed a check-up – so I thought I'd just head to St Mary's Hospital on Praed Street in Paddington. They theoretically had my medical records – although I think I may well have been registered in most of the dozen hospitals in North West London. However, as I walked towards St Mary's that day I felt weird – and I collapsed in the doorway of the hospital. It was very simple really. I was malnourished – less than six stone again and my system had gone into toxic shock. This was something that would reoccur with more and more frequency over the next two years. In fact, I know at a later date St Thomas's refused to treat me because I had pancreatitis and continued to drink.

I came to briefly and said I had to go home – I was already craving a drink and a hit. It was July the 7th and the reason I know the date is because it was the day of the London Tube bombings. Anyway, I slipped into unconsciousness again and it was a day or two later before I came to again. I had drips and tubes both in and out of every orifice – and it was horrendous.

I was on methadone and ended up staying as an in-patient there for almost two months, mainly because I was homeless. Vivian's sister came to visit me initially and for a small fee would bring me a bottle of vodka every day. The hospital assigned me a social worker and she was working on getting me a flat in Admiral House in Victoria. It was an awful kip and I wasn't mad about the location but at the time I was intensely grateful for it. I became a sort of night patient for a while. I'd tootle off every morning after breakfast and wander about the town, return for lunch, have a chat with the duty nurse, off again having a look around the shops, nipping at vodka all the time – although clever enough to keep it under their radar – and then return before curfew to St Mary's. I got to quite like it; it was a safe routine and people were kind. I suppose I became somewhat

263

institutionalised. It wouldn't have been hard – my mind was a blank most of the time anyway. I was simply existing, you really couldn't call it living, but it was easeful in a way. But of course it couldn't last. Now the poor hospital staff – they tried their best to feed me up and by the time I left them I did succeed in putting up a stone so I was up to seven stone. They got me counselling and I said, "Oh great, yeah, of course I'll go!" – and never went to any of it.

When they finally discharged me I stood outside that hospital and thought. What now, Rebecca? What's left? It was 2005, my father was finally dead and I was quite sure none of the rest of my family wanted anything to do with me. Christ, I hardly wanted anything to do with myself. I was homeless, penniless and say what you want about England but by God their Welfare State looked after me. And that is how a nation should be judged – on how it treats those least able to care for themselves.

The first night I spent in Admiral House I had no furniture – my furniture cheque hadn't come through. I lay on the floor in a corner of the living-room with my old fur coat about me. I don't think I slept – just lay there wondering at the shithole my life had become.

I became a complete recluse in my own home.

There isn't a lot to tell over the next two years: a sad litany of alcohol, hospital, more alcohol, more hospital.

September 2005 to October 2007 were the worst years of my life. I cannot explain to you how deep and dark and unendingly despairing I was. Words cannot describe it, but there is one image that might explain. In the Fassbender film, *Hunger*, one of the characters on the dirty protest in the H-Blocks in the North paints a sort of vortex in his own excrement on the wall. That's what my life was like: a deep, shitty unending hell.

I had kicked heroin but I could never see my way past the bottom of a vodka bottle and I thought I never would. The ambulance came for me at least twice a month, called by Gabriel or someone else. My weight dropped again to under the six stone, they'd check me in, nourish me for a day or two, mainly rehydrating me, then I'd discharge myself and go back to the flat via Tesco's for the vodka. I did a stint in the mental health hospital – Gordon's – once even standing outside on the window ledge of the room I was in, trying to will myself to jump. It was staff in the office block across the road who spotted me and reported it. Many, many times after that I would wish I had taken that leap. I was living on social security and I'm not proud of that. I had always tried to support myself until those last few years but I had become incapable of doing anything at that stage.

I budgeted only for fags and booze. I had it down to a fine art. I would wake at 7a.m., walk for five minutes to the 24hr Tesco and buy a litre bottle of vodka and twenty cigarettes and that's more or less what I lived on for the day. I'd have the occasional good day where I'd be a little uplifted and if an old (non-drug using) friend called I might let them in. But if I was in a bad mood I quite simply wouldn't answer the door. Just sit on the sofa wishing they'd stop pressing the bloody doorbell. If I did let them in, I wouldn't want to give my visitor any of my vodka so would hide my bottle and say, "Oh, I've just poured the last of it into my glass." Then the friend might volunteer to go and get another. Oh, joy!

Gabriel called regularly and I became quite dependent on him both for company and to bring me booze. I would drink and pass out, come to and drink again and fall asleep some more. Oblivion is what I wanted. Anything was better than my life.

I always tried to make sure there was a drop left in the bottle before I fell asleep – so I would have one to hold me together until Tesco opened at 7a.m. But the number of times I woke up at four in the morning with no fags and no booze! I'd be in bits, shaking, and I'd be afraid I wouldn't make to Tesco's without shitting or wetting myself. My system was in complete meltdown and both occurrences were regular. On the day my monthly money was due, I would try and get dolled up and go to town, maybe buy myself something to wear – very high street, not my lovely designer gear – not even shop-lifted designer any more, which is where a lot of my clothes had come from in recent years. Sometimes Gabriel would appear and one week, in October 2007, I rowed with him, telling him he only ever turned up when I was expecting cash. He left in a huff and it was fuck him, didn't need him either. I decided to go out anyway. I must have looked like Bette Davis as Baby

Jane Hudson. I'd no money that night – the giro was due the following day – but I would go into Soho and blag drink off someone and sure after a drink or two I could wheedle drink from anyone.

On the Wednesday my money arrived and I went to the pub across the road and there were two men at the bar and they bought me drink for a while.

Then they started to torment me. "Show us your tits!"

I went mad. "C'mon outside and I'll fight you, I'll fight you for the right for you to look at my tits!" I was a snarling harpy, the worst I'd ever been.

The bar manager called the police to have me taken away – more for my own safety than anything else. I'd say the two guys were going to kill me. It was yet another lowest point. That point where you either have to keep doing what you're doing and die or by some miracle claw your way back out to the real world. I was taken to the police station, fingerprinted for the first (and last) time, photographed and put in a cell. I was miserable. Terrified and miserable. How had I let it get to this? The duty doctor came and talked to me. I promised I would go looking for help. But this was the clincher for me – the beginning of the end, only not quite yet. The doctor warned me if I did not do something soon then I would be dead in a very short time. My liver, kidneys, my whole system would just pack up.

And as I was promising all this to the doctor and the policemen I could visualise the vodka bottle at home. I knew I couldn't go to the pub again. But no-one could stop me drinking at home. That is how devious alcohol can make the mind – it is always there, waiting to pounce and reclaim you. I started to drink as soon as I got home – all promises forgotten or rather put off until the bottle was empty. I rang Gabriel to try to apologise but he wasn't returning my calls. I had really hurt him – I can be vicious when I'm lonely and lash out in anger.

On the Friday of that week when I woke from my semi-coma, I decided: '*Right, Rebecca, do yourself up and go downtown. And keep your word to the doctor . . . but next week. When you're more able for it.*' I had tried to be admitted to treatment centres in London on a few occasions but once I was told we'll take you in two weeks! Of course by the time the fortnight was up my nerve had gone and I was back on the merry-go-round of boozing.

To this day I do not know what happened next. I was alone in this squalid little flat and I woke up on the floor. I was in awful pain – but all of me seemed to be in pain – I couldn't isolate it. I could see the bottle of vodka where I'd left it and shifted, or tried to shift up on my arm to reach it. I was kept down by the most horrendous pain all up my arm I looked to see why the pain was worse and my arm had ballooned up. I must have broken it when I fell. But I didn't remember falling. And I looked like I had been out – a huge chunk of the evening was missing and it was the longest blackout since coming to in Amsterdam in 2002. I lay there for a while crying – I had become a tramp, happy with the down-and-outs around Victoria. I was so thin, wearing kids' clothes and at times Gabriel had to lift me into the bath because I was too weak to climb in. I felt a calm falling on me and when I opened my eyes again it was like a new life had taken over me. Some higher power. I got to my feet and took the vodka bottle with my good hand and poured the last dregs of it down the sink. That was the last time but one that I came even close to drinking alcohol.

I rang a support group and they were to send someone but they couldn't find my place. I knew there was a meeting in the psychiatric hospital nearby (where I had already done two stints over the course of the last five years) but I was still kind of drunk – my system still full of vodka. I knew there was a meeting in Knightsbridge at 10a.m. the next morning. I was half afraid to sleep in case my resolve went. So I sat up most of the night, TV on, staring blankly at it. Still in agony with the arm, I made my way to the meeting in this posh part of London. I was starting to shake and must have looked like an awful wreck – I hadn't showered, God knows when I had washed my hair last – I had last night's make-up half on. I walked into this room full of well-dressed beautiful people and on the way in I met a lovely American lady who proved to be my saviour and she took me from that meeting to another. She gave me money for cigarettes and I was in bits with tremors at this stage and two women took me around the corner to the hospital and waited while I got my arm bandaged. Then I went back to another meeting that night and as I heard story after story and listened, really listened, I realised I had found the right place to be.

I have never taken a drink since and I will not drink today or today or today.

I got a sponsor, I started to make commitments and carry them out, I helped out at meetings and people could see me getting stronger every day. I helped out around Christmas.

Even Gabriel looked at me one day and said, "You know – I think you're going to do it this time. I think you're going to make it."

I literally just grew every day and took every day on its own merits. In January 2008 I decided to rechristen myself – rebrand Rebecca. I wanted a new surname, something classy. I had carried the surname of someone who hadn't cared enough to hang around for my second birthday, hadn't cared enough to make sure I didn't get raped by bastards and fucked over by life. So no – I didn't owe Tallon any dues. I thought about it – I'd always loved Olivia De Havilland and Louis Walsh used to say that I was like her. "Gone With The Bloody Wind," he'd say when I would throw a wobbly about something. I felt there was more Scarlett O'Hara than Melanie Wilkes in me but it stuck in my head, a connection to a good time in my life. Rebecca De Havalland – it had a nice ring with a slight spelling change. A name I had chosen to go with the path I had chosen in life. So Rebecca De Havalland was deed-polled into existence and I think that was the day that the final 'real' Rebecca was born – the Rebecca I had wanted to be since June 1958.

I had one more hurdle to leap though. I felt that although I was coming up towards six months' sobriety that my recovery from alcohol wasn't honest. I knew I wasn't being honest. I was still skirting around things, glossing over them, afraid that people wouldn't accept me if they saw all the warts – I found some of the episodes in my life hard to accept myself. I hadn't, for example, told anyone in the meetings about Ava. How could I do that – or not do that? How could I deny her? Perhaps ashamed that I had accepted Andrea's and society's decisions and stayed out of her life? I don't know, I never tried to analyse it before. I just couldn't seem to prize the lid off that fucking pain – I was afraid it would engulf me.

It was St Patrick's week March 2008, the week before Easter. I went to a meeting in South Kensington and people were congratulating me on how well I was doing and something inside me snapped. I had to get out of there, I could not take the pressure of not being truthful. I knew I wasn't being honest, that my recovery was not good recovery. I had seen people being honest and I wasn't, I thought, capable of it. I had a load of anti-depressants in the house and I bought myself a half bottle of vodka. I was never going to be able to do this – this recovery shit. Doing this bridge to 'normal living'. I was in so much fucking pain and I needed it to go away now – I was back to where I had been after my first attempt at recovery in Belfast. I knew what falling off the wagon meant this time and who was I fooling? Everyone who had ever cared anything about me had disowned me if I was drinking; so I planned my suicide.

I would take myself off to the bright blue yonder on medication and a last drink. As I was organising myself it was sort of comforting; it reminded me of getting tinfoil etc ready for a rock of crack. I opened the bottle of vodka and opened the pills, I must have had about forty 50mg amitriptyline laid out in handfuls, and started to take them with gulps of water, they started to come back up and I forced them down. They seemed to have an almost immediate effect and I could feel myself getting woozy and starting to pass out. I started to panic and lifted the vodka bottle and put it down, picking up my mobile instead and texting 'HELP' to Gabriel.

When I came to I was on a life-support machine in hospital, tubes down my throat. Gabriel had been nearby and had broken the door down to get to me, immediately calling an ambulance. The paramedics had tried to resuscitate me and my heart had stopped in the ambulance, forcing them to administer an adrenaline injection to my heart.

I was in the intensive care unit of the hospital for a number of days and the nurses were gentle and kind with me, the doctor a little more brutal.

"This is your last chance," he said. "One more drink, one more brush with drugs and you're dead. Your liver shows signs of cirrhosis, your pancreas cannot take any more. If you stop – now – if you stop and never start again, then you might live."

It was blunt and I think if he had said that to me a week earlier I would quite simply have closed my eyes and died. But obviously some part of me had chosen life.

However, whatever had made me text Gabriel for help, whatever part of me had decided I had to stay alive here for some other reason, seemed to have gone into retreat again.

I was kept under close observation for a few days and then discharged. Jesus. I felt rejected again. Was I going to have to keep doing this? I didn't realise that they had me on suicide watch and Gabriel was part of it. People in the area and people from my support group were all keeping a close eye on me.

A couple of days later someone from the team saw me heading for Tesco's looking mad as a brush. She approached me and tried to get me to go down to Gordon's Mental Health Hospital with her for "a chat and a cup it tea".

"No. I have to get my vodka," I said.

She knew she had to prevent that. She persuaded me to walk down towards the hospital with her as I moaned about how terrible I felt. We ran into Deb, a lady who had befriended me and who was to play a large part in my recovery. Deb came down with us too and the women talked to me the whole time. When we got to the hospital and headed upstairs, I realised they were taking me to the lock-up ward. I went ballistic and had to be physically restrained by nurses and aides. Complete breakdown.

For the first, and I hope last, time in my life I was sectioned for 72 hours for my own safety. I was on constant watch – which literally meant I could not even use the toilet on my own. Those who have near-death experiences say that your whole life flashes before your eyes. I don't know what term you would use to describe my experience during that sectioned period but everything – everything that had happened to me in my life – to all my personalities, to Eamon, the abused and institutionalised kid, to Manic Ross, to Rebecca in all her guises – I relived all of it. At one stage they were even wondering if I was bi-polar. I wasn't, thank God.

I let it all out. I was in Gordon's for almost six weeks and it was what is euphemistically called 'a complete breakdown', but also the start of a recovery. Deb came to visit me every day. She is Catholic and she was a huge source of comfort and strength to me. After the first three days the medical team let me out to my support group meetings and I started to make that honest recovery that had so far eluded me. To this day I am continuing in that honest recovery. I let everything out, everything – and realised that was all I had ever needed to do. Ironically I think this is the first time that the medics in Gordon's would have kept me forever. I had done three or four spells there over the years and they had always released me fairly quickly. This 'breakdown' was so complete I think they thought I would require hospitalisation for life. But it was the first time for many, many years that I really felt I would be able to start my life anew.

I met Sara who has become my sponsor and has helped me to make a good recovery and she is still a good and dear friend. Deb took me to Lourdes after a few months and it was in Lourdes that I felt that desire to drink, that awful nagging sensation, being lifted from me. Our Lady, always my friend even though in my darkest days I had sometimes worried she had abandoned me, had granted me this comfort and for that I will be eternally grateful.

I was truly on the path to wholeness again.

19

Hannah and her Sisters

I think the surrendering of my fate on the day I started honest recovery to whatever power it was that wanted me to live has ultimately been the making of the human being I am today. My happy early childhood days in Granard with my family and these last two years of my life have been my most positive and uplifting years. Funny, with that uplifting positivity comes a strange fear. The same fear one has as a child. That 'what if'.

As children we depend on the adults about us to make our lives safe. Children expect adults to control their world and will bide by adult rules because they appear to work and should make their lives run in a peaceful and consistent manner. I no longer try to control my life. Like a child I place my life in the hands of my higher power, for me Our Lady, every morning and she guides me through the day. At night I thank her for getting me safely through another day. I still worry, will make mistakes and slip into old ways of thinking, trying to control things over which I have no control. Sometimes I want to put the brakes on in sheer fear at the wonder and speed of some of the things that are happening. There are other times when I try to speed up things I'm impatient with, that aren't happening fast enough for my ever-racing mind. But I'm learning – changing what I can, accepting what I cannot and most importantly learning to see the difference between the two.

It hasn't all been plain sailing and there have been times I was tempted to drink but I have come to the ultimate realisation that I cannot control my drinking. I think in some secret recess of my brain I thought that one day I would be able to, but once any addiction has you in its grasp it does not let go easily. The easy way – the only way – to give up drink is not to drink. There is no other way.

I had applied for a transfer from the flat in Admiral House and I got my transfer to a lovely little flat in Carnaby Street – ironically back in Soho – but this time my life in Soho was to be so, so different. I got myself a little dog, my darling Coco, and set about making a complete and honest recovery from my life of addiction. This is where a trio of angels came into my life. Don't worry, I haven't lost it. These are real live angels, all the way from Bermondsey. Angels with London accents, lovely smiles, big hearts and honest souls. Hannah and her sisters Keeley and Suzanne – 'Suzy Q'. These three women and their mum Sandy were to become my dearest friends at a time when I never needed friends more. They opened their hearts and homes to me. Hannah lived upstairs from me in the house in Carnaby Street and we became friends very quickly. Hannah introduced me to Keeley, Suzie Q and their mum and they all became my 'sisters'. Bit by bit it grew. Hannah would help me around any fears I had about confrontation – she was endlessly patient and kind. We all had such fun together and I would do their hair for them, talk to them about their boyfriends, their lives, ordinary normal everyday stuff. I was healing.

I was still suffering from anxiety attacks and panic attacks and would occasionally become reclusive, not answering the door when the girls would come calling.

But Hannah wouldn't give up without a battle: "I know you're in there, babe. C'mon, Rebecca – open up!"

And I would and in this way every day I got a little stronger, my anxiety lessened and my sense of purpose started to grow. I got used to normal living – to telling the truth about how I felt and watching, relieved, as people didn't reject me for this truth. From the age of about three I had hidden my gender, then from seven the abuse – as I aged I became expert at hiding everything and anything until I didn't even know who I was. Now here I was slowly unburdening myself of all those deceptions and becoming the person I had always been at heart.

Hannah says that for that first year of my recovery I

reminded her of a rabbit caught in headlights, so scared of everything. Hannah looks at me now, my strength and all I am about to take on, and shakes her head in admiration. In this transformation Hannah has played no small part – I thank you, my friend.

A funny aside. The girls were fascinated with all my little statues of Our Lady and St Bernadette and St Therese and I explained about the Blessed Virgin and how she had appeared in different places like Lourdes and Knock and Medjugorje at different times. They thought she sounded lovely and wondered why they didn't have her in their religion (they're Church of England). *The Tudors* with Jonathan Rhys Meyers was a popular series on television at the time and I explained about Henry the Eight getting thick with the Pope because the Pope would not annul his marriage to Queen Katherine. So Henry set up his own church and made himself the head of it so he could divorce the Queen and marry Anne Boleyn. My Bermondsey angels were horrified that their religion had come about because of some cheating man! I bought them all Miraculous Medals and they wear them all the time. One night Suzy Q was getting ready to go out and she had a top on that wouldn't look right with the medal. She winked at me, then showed me where she had stuck Our Lady to the inside of her wrist with blue tack to keep her safe when she was on the razz! I think the Catholic Church should put me on commission for proselytising

As part of my recovery I had to attain certain goals and as I achieved each one my resolve became stronger and stronger. I started to use a computer and quickly got the hang of internet, e-mailing and Facebook. I found Lucy on Facebook and tentatively sent out a feeler. She answered me immediately and told me to ring her.

When she answered the phone my first question was: "Are you still talking to me?"

"Of course I'm talking to you. I just can't handle you drinking."

I told her about this recovery, how I was sure if I stayed true to the tenets of my support group that I would overcome my alcoholism – today. I think she recognised a new strength in me because we chatted for ages about a lot of things. Mum had been ill and had been diagnosed with Alzheimer's and we discussed her care for a while. She filled me in on the doings of family and friends. It was lovely and it became a regular occurrence that we would ring each other and chat, something that had been missing from our relationship for a long, long time. I put all my resentments down and it is that, that dumping of baggage, that has saved me.

Hannah used to go up to this beauty school to get her legs waxed and I went up with her one day, I was impressed with the set-up and made enquires about mature students. They said they took them and I applied and was accepted to do my NVQ Level II. Not only did I go on to complete the course, sitting in with sixteen and seventeen-year-olds but I sat an exam –

my first! – and passed with flying colours. I was extraordinarily proud of myself.

I was content with my life. I had little or no money; I was living on benefits, but for the first time in my life it didn't bother me. I had sufficient onto the day and for the most part that was enough. I volunteered to act as secretary at one of the meetings I went to, I walked the dog, I visited friends, I prayed. A simple life, a peaceful life. I ran into old friends from Ireland occasionally and we would laugh about the mad times we had in our clubbing days.

I undertook to assist at meetings all over London that winter and I remember walking through Hyde Park on Christmas morning 2008, talking to Lucy on the phone and smiling and laughing. After my call I walked proud and tall and thought, '*This is happiness.*' I was achieving things, setting goals and meeting them. I was living.

Family started to visit me again in London and I applied for and was awarded a bigger apartment in a new purpose-built block in Victoria with a Housing Association. I was meant to get the keys in February 2009 but there was a delay and when Lucy came to visit in March I was still in the smaller place in Carnaby Street. I was so nervous. But I needn't have been – it was lovely, really lovely. My niece Sam was due her second baby that spring – I was a gran-aunt and everything became very family-orientated. My college course was coming to an end and I applied to the London School of Fashion to do an access course with a view to doing

Beauty Journalism. I was accepted and was to start the course in September 2009 – I swear I don't think I was ever as pleased with myself. I was grounded, I had a safe place to live, my family were in my life, I had good friends and it looked like I might have a chance of a career still in the beauty industry.

20

Full Circle

In June 2009 friends and family clubbed together to fly me home for my 52nd birthday. I was excited but nervous. I had messed up so badly so many times. I had started to trust myself in London, to believe I was worthy of a decent life but I worried that I wouldn't feel the same in Ireland. I genuinely thought I would live out the rest of my life in London. Gabriel was to come with me but he pulled out at the last minute.

I was so nervous when I got to Dublin Airport. I remembered the last time I had been there in 2005 – and I didn't even remember it. I think if I was ever to drink again it would have been then – it was huge pressure on me, but I took it and I didn't drink.

So home I came and it was lovely. I met up with everyone.

Mum hadn't got too bad and was still able to recognise me.

"You look lovely," she said. "Your hair and clothes, haven't you great style? Isn't it a pity we can't do anything about that auld voice?"

We laughed and it was good to make my peace with her. She doesn't know me now most of the time and I'm glad that I was able to laugh with her and say goodbye before that happened. I stayed with friends in Fitzwilliam Square, Dublin – Pat and Laura – for a few days. I attended meetings around the city, shopped, met family for lunch and dinner and generally enjoyed myself. I met a friend Meg for tea in the Shelbourne one evening and she took me to the nightclub Krystle in Harcourt Street for the first time so I might see 2009's crop of socialites and top models. I was horrified at the over-processed hair and orange tan make-up. I couldn't believe these girls were Dublin's top models and we sat criticising for the night. These girls had potential but in their current state they wouldn't last two seconds on the London fashion scene.

I ran into Michael Wright in the city one day. Michael would have dropped into Chaos, the club I had briefly run twenty years before in Dublin and I would have known him from Dublin's social scene over the years. Michael couldn't get over how well I looked and we went for a coffee and he told me about the Wright Venue, a new nightclub he was opening up in Swords in County Dublin. It was modelled on some of the London and European city clubs and was a totally new experience for Dublin. There were to be several floors and stages in it and it sounded fantastic. He asked if I'd come over for the opening the following month and I said I'd love to.

Another guy asked me to chair a meeting in a Dublin suburb later in the week but I told him I really ought to get back to London. I had got the keys to my new flat in Victoria just before I came to Dublin and, although I had moved in, I hadn't had any time to enjoy my new space. The guy who asked me, pleaded with me – he thought my story so inspirational that it would do a lot of people a lot of good. I thought about something Sara my sponsor had said about never turning down a request for service unless I really had to – that good always came of giving service freely. I rang Hannah in London and asked her to continue looking after Coco and she agreed so I changed my flight and stayed on to chair the meeting.

Michael Wright heard I was still in Dublin and he rang me and asked me to meet him as he wanted to run something by me. I went out to the Wright Venue in Swords later that week and was very impressed with the club. Michael thought I would really help draw a crowd if I would front his hostessing squad. I wouldn't have to so much as lift a glass, just wander around playing 'Lady V' ('V' for 'Venue') – maybe go out on some of the buses they were using to bring people in from all over the city. I wasn't sure. I thought the Wright Venue was a super venue but I didn't know if I wanted back into that life and I also felt I was too old and raddled. I joked that if I could get a faceful of Botox I'd think about it.

"I'll pay for it," he said.

"Get lost! You're not serious," I said.

"I am," he said. "You were the best hostess I ever saw and I want the best for the Venue. It's an investment in the club."

"Okay, okay. Let me think about it."

I went home and thought. It was only going to be two nights a week, the money was good and I could do it for a couple of months – until my college course started. My flat in London was safe. Michael said the Venue would look after my accommodation costs in Dublin initially and I'd get a Botox lift as well. It was a no-brainer. I had no fear of being lured back into drinking. I was quite sure that that part of my life was over.

So I went back to London to sort out clothes and, of course, my darling Coco, and have my face done.

I had the Botox sessions and I swear I had absolutely no facial movement after them. I had arranged to do secretary at one of my meetings and I went along without any ability to express any kind of a reaction to anything. I couldn't open my mouth beyond a stiff-upper-lip yes or no. It was an extremely intense meeting with a lot of heavy stories and there were a lot of people that I didn't know particularly well.

I started to get a little self-conscious and was worried that people might think I was staring at them so just before the meeting ended I piped up; "Please excuse my appearance. I'm not being rude when I stare at you. I've just had Botox and can't move." The place erupted. I think it was the first time I heard an extended round of laughter and applause at one of those meetings. It certainly broke the tension and lifted everyone's mood!

All my friends in London were thrilled for me – my life seemed to have nowhere to go but up: family, friends and now a good job! Over the next two months I was over and back between Dublin and London, getting procedures done on my face, rehearsing in the club with the other hostesses and organising costumes. The Wright Venue was putting me up in the hotel beside The Venue but it was a lonely time and I was always glad of the breaks in London. Eventually The Venue agreed to pay a deposit and a month's rent on an apartment in Malahide and I decided to sublet the apartment in London so at least that wasn't a drain on my finances.

Malahide was lovely but I was never used to that type of suburban living and I just could not settle in the apartment. I was so busy in The Venue initially that it didn't matter – there were over 500 staff in the place on different shifts etcetera and people were always coming and going. We had a couple of practice nights and then came opening night and Lady V went down a bomb. I would go over to Malahide and into town on the WV bus, welcoming punters on, and then stalk about or do one of my stage routines when we went back to the club. I had never lost it, that ability to switch on this persona. It was quite simple – sort of just wandering about as if all these revellers were interlopers in my house – being photographed with those who wanted photos etcetera – but I bloody hated it at this stage in my life. It was the means to an end though.

I got very friendly with one of the girls there, Lianne, and as the weeks went by I told her my *scéal*.

On the August Bank Holiday weekend 2009, Lianne walked in and I noticed she'd had her hair cut and commented on it. Lianne is mixed race and has beautiful kinky hair.

"Sure, I could have done that for you – I'm well used to those aul Afros!" I quipped.

"Oh, yeah! I forgot, wasn't your wife – *uuugghh,* that is so gross – wasn't she mixed race too?" she wrinkled her nose at me, laughing.

"She was – still is, I'm sure," I rejoined.

"Ava here is quarter mixed too – you know Ava, my pal, the girl who sits in the booth beside yours, the one you're always dancing with?" (The booths were little rest stops for the staff throughout the club.)

"Is she? No, she's not – is she? That little one in the next booth? Is she Ava . . .?"

"Yeah . . . that's her name.'

I thought about it but no – I mean, my Ava was almost twenty-nine – this little Ava was nearer to twenty . . . it was just a coincidence.

"Don't tell me now Ava's mother's name is Andrea," I said half-joking, half getting scared.

"Yes. Yes. Oh, Jesus!" Lianne had gone pale.

"Don't tell me her dad, her step-dad's name is James Boland?" I could hardly get the words out.

"Yes," Lianne was whispering and her eyes were filling with tears.

"She's my daughter. Oh, Sweet Mother of Divine God. Ava's my daughter." I felt dizzy and had to sit down. I was shaking from head to foot.

"But you weren't Eamon Tallon. You were Ross Tallon!"

As Lianne said it, I could see she knew the answer – she was just trying to dissuade herself from believing in this miracle.

"Ross was only ever a hairdressing name. I am Eamon Tallon from Granard in Longford."

The club was about to open. Lianne had the keys in her hand to open all the tills, I was standing there in a swimsuit and feathers about to go out on the bus to welcome in all the Bank Holiday weekend revellers. I thought I was going to throw up and Lianne had to help me to the toilets where I calmed down . . . and put on my professional face and performed.

I had moved out of the apartment in Malahide and was staying with friends in Balbriggan by now and Lianne came out to the house the following day. Ava wasn't working in Wrights that weekend. She was away in Wexford with her husband and her daughter. I had a four-year-old granddaughter – Hazel! I was so thrilled, a grown daughter and a little granddaughter!

Lianne knew Ava's family history – the women are close friends and have been for a number of years.

"It's weird," said Lianne. "We were watching you perform last week and Ava said to me 'Isn't Lady V amazing?' and I answered, 'Wouldn't it be great if your dad was as accomplished and professional as that – maybe he is somewhere in the world?'"

Lianne had contacted Ava and told her she had to see her as soon as she got back to Dublin. They met up on the Tuesday after the Bank Holiday weekend and Lianne told her the story. Ava's first reaction was funny.

"But Lady V doesn't even like me! I asked her to go for a cigarette the other day and she wouldn't, she said she was busy."

She had a lot to think about and she wasn't due into work for the next week. I told Michael Wright and he nearly fainted. He couldn't believe it. What were the bloody chances of that happening? Once I was okay to work he was happy to let me stay until Ava and I had discussed things – if we discussed things. My mind wasn't on the job though and I could see the General Manager of the Venue was getting pissed off with me.

The next night Ava was due on I was in early, costumed up and sitting in the open-air bar having a cigarette when she arrived out to do the same.

"Alright?" She smiled shyly at me.

"Alright." I smiled back.

The rest is family history and not fully my story to tell. Ava and I became quickly close and she gradually introduced me to her husband and my granddaughter and to her in-laws. Ava has inherited my love of fashion and she has the same eye I have for make-up, hair and clothes. She was working as assistant buyer for a major fashion brand then, as well as a few shifts at the Wright Venue, but I don't think either job had matched her expectations. She was fascinated with my stories of the model industry and confessed that running or having her own model agency had always been her dream.

The Wright Venue wasn't working out for me. I wasn't comfortable now with Ava seeing me as this invented creature Lady V, whom men seemed to think had no problem with them pulling at any part of her body that took their fancy. The General Manager suggested I might be happier elsewhere and I agreed. I started to think about the modelling game and had a look around.

People thought I was mad – rushing things in an uncertain financial climate – but I could see an opening for beautiful classy models and for a variety of models – children, mature, event as well as high-end fashion. I moved into a tiny office in Temple Bar and started to get a few models together. It snowballed – I wasn't the only one who could see an opening. Ava was put on a three-day week with her permanent job and she rowed in behind me.

Now top-class photographers and hair stylists have signed my girls. I have let my flat in London – the flat I fought for and loved – go. We moved De Havalland

Event and Model Management back to Baggot Street, very close to where Tallon Models had been twenty years previously and the future looks bright for our family business. My family. My daughter and granddaughter. At last.

21

The Last Word

And so my circle is complete. I am back in Dublin, back building a career for myself and my daughter. I am in contact with my family in Granard. These last twenty-two months have been the most amazing, sometimes frightening and frustrating, but almost always fulfilling months of my life. My life to date, I think you will agree, has been a rollercoaster and I am now on the home stretch of that coaster and hopefully the ride is slowing down a little. I am trying to take things slowly, day by day, hour by hour, minute by minute. Living in the now, or trying to. Although I don't know. Stuff just seems to happen to me, I am being constantly tested – they say it makes you stronger. I believe it does but there are days . . !

Let me tell you about Christmas 2009.

I had been back to London for a quick visit and planned to fly home to Dublin on the morning of

Christmas Eve. I was to spend time with Ava, her husband Brian and of course little Hazel. Ava had even suggested I help her "put out Santa" for Hazel after she had gone to bed. I couldn't believe it, I was overjoyed. Here I was getting the chance to share in something, something really, really special, with my daughter and her little family. The absence of those special nights, special moments, were absences that had killed me every Christmas, birthday and every other special day of Ava's life. And now I was getting a chance to do it. Nothing – nothing – was going to stop me.

Having read this far you all know how determined I can be. But by God was I tested!

As you know by now, I don't 'do' mornings. I never have been and never will be a morning person. I don't click into life until after noon every day, so in general if I'm not working I try to organise my life around later starts. But nothing was going to mess with my Christmas Eve. So, after running around London for a couple of days earlier that week – remember, I had only gone home to Ireland for a 'short visit' six months earlier – on Christmas Eve morning I got up at five and was in the airport by seven. The flight was due to leave at nine and under normal circumstances I should have been back in Dublin city centre by eleven, or at least before noon. I had already agreed to be out at Ava's house in Dublin by three.

It was snowing in London and icy in Dublin but the flight was only a little late in boarding. Good, all was going well – Our Lady was on duty, I thought. We were all strapped in, the stewardesses in their seats and the plane had started to manoeuvre its way to the runway when it stopped. Five minutes went by, that grew to ten minutes and then to a muttering-filled fifteen minutes. Finally the pilot's voice came on over the intercom and apologised. Apparently another plane had skidded on attempting to depart so for safety reasons our plane had to wait until the runway was cleared of snow and ice. Fine – thank you, Our Lady – keep up the good work.

We sat there for almost two hours. *Two hours!!* I was getting edgy, very edgy. I hadn't had a cigarette for three hours and I was dying for one. I wondered had Our Lady gone for an early *and very long* lunch. The stewardesses were going up and down the aisle with the drinks trolley and people were loosening up.

I could have one. Nobody would know, I thought. But I didn't take a drink – because I would know and it is primarily for me that I don't drink. I'm not boastful or proud or anything like that about it. It's very simple. I am an alcoholic. I don't drink. I don't drink to save myself. So I took deep breaths of recirculated cabin air and let me tell you it is no substitute for a lungful of nicotine!

The plane finally took off, one hour after it was supposed to have landed in Dublin, so I was running two hours late at this stage. When I got through Dublin Airport I almost sprinted out to the bus-stop. I got on the first bus and set about trying to contact Ava and my young friend Julien who had been staying in my two-roomed Dublin apartment to look after Lulu, the little dog I got to replace my darling Coco who had disappeared from a friend's house where I had been staying in Balbriggan – I assumed she was stolen because she didn't tend to stray. The flippin' battery on my mobile was almost dead and I knew it would run out. I approached the bus-driver and asked him if he had somewhere I could plug it in. God bless you, sir, whoever you were because I would have been lost without you! He very, very kindly plugged it in to some outlet on the control panel and standing there beside him I made my phone calls.

Julien was distraught when I finally got hold of him. He's French and speaks the most beautifully accented English. Julien had overslept on Christmas Eve morning and only woke when he heard the front door bang. It was only when he was ready to leave the building that he discovered that the photographer who has offices upstairs from me had pulled out the door after him and Chubb-locked it. I had no Chubb key! I was supposed to have borrowed the photographer's and have one cut. He must have assumed we were finished up for Christmas so he security-locked the door. There is a long drop from the office window down to the courtyard – Julien had a look and decided if he could lower himself partway he could jump the last bit.

I'd love to have actually seen the next bit, because it sounds so like something out of the *Pink Panther*. I can picture Peter Sellers as Inspector Clouseau doing something like it! Julien found some discarded telephone cabling and, using his obviously fertile imagination, tied one end to the banisters and extended the lead out the window. Remember this young man was already an hour late for work in a shop in Dundrum Shopping Centre on the southside of Dublin. He hoisted himself onto the windowsill and looked over. '*I can do this,*' he thought. I can only assume that Julien must have imagined he was Spiderman or some other superhero when he was a child and hoped his 'super powers' were still with him. Of course the telephone cabling wire gave way and poor old Julien ended up in a heap in the courtyard with a badly damaged ankle.

So when he took my call from the bus into the city he was in hospital – where he had spent the previous five hours.

"Oh no! You poor thing," I said. Then, realising how this incident affected me, I squawked, "Oh Julien! No! How am I going to get in?"

"Ziz is wat I am telling you, Reebekka. Ze man, ze photographer. He has locked ze door." Poor Julien! Poor me! I thought it was time Our Lady got off her tea break.

I tried Ava next. She had checked the airport's website and, when she saw the flight had been delayed, had been trying to contact me to tell me not to go in to Baggot Street, that she would pick me up at the airport. I was almost in Dublin City at this stage. I had Ava's and Hazel's presents with me. I had hoped to have time to get Ava's husband a gift but time was too tight. So I got off the bus and took a taxi out to Ava's house. Fifty euro! I was never as broke in all my life and there I was spending € 50 on taxis. It didn't matter. I have never, ever known such joy as I felt that Christmas Eve night. Our Lady was forgiven (we never fall out for long) and bar the day Ava was born it was the happiest evening of my life.

Everything that had happened that day. All the bad things that happened to me all my depressed nights, nights of crying and wondering why, why, why me. They all went. I was in the living-room of my daughter's house opening gifts and laughing and smiling and just simply being myself with them all. I cannot describe how wonderful it felt. It was absolutely the best, most contented and consistent high I have ever experienced. Hazel was so excited about Santa and of course we adults almost believed in him ourselves by the time her bedtime came! When she was fast asleep Ava's husband took all the presents from their hidey holes and we *oohed* and *aahed* over them as we imagined Hazel's little face when she saw all the lovely gifts the magical man in the red suit had left her.

"What's wrong?" asked Ava.

It's amazing. She is so instinctual when it comes to me, that parent/child bond is still there even though it had been left untouched for years. She knows me so well. She had noticed I was edgy. To be honest, I was worried about getting back to town. It was twelve o'clock Christmas Eve and I needed to take a taxi from North County Dublin all the way across the county to South County Dublin to collect the Chubb key from the photographer at his home. The taxi would have to wait for me and then take me home to Baggot Street. I thought it would probably cost me over a hundred euro, money I could ill-afford.

"Nothing," I said.

Ava looked at me. "Tell me. I know something is worrying you."

So I told her I was worried I wouldn't be able to get a taxi. Do you know what she did? Aren't our kids just so great?

"Take my car," she said. "Sure we can travel in Brian's car over the holiday."

God bless the sweet child! So it was after midnight when I left Ava's house and headed towards the Southside in bitter, bitter cold – wind and snow and ice. The roads in Dublin had all changed in the ten years I'd been away so between that, the road conditions and exhaustion, I suppose my driving wasn't the best. But I couldn't believe it when a police car sirened and blue-lighted me and indicated I should pull in.

A young female Garda came to the window of my car.

"You were driving a little erratically, madam," she said.

"I'm old and bloody terrified!" I rejoined.

She laughed. "Seriously, you were all over the road so I'm afraid I'll have to breathalyse you – any objections?'

I roared laughing. "Please, please, please do!" I said. "I have waited twenty-two months for someone to say that – breathalyse me by all means!"

The Garda went back to the police car and came back with a little breath-testing kit.

"Why have you been waiting for this for twenty-two months?" she asked, smiling.

"I'm in recovery for that length of time," I said, "and I'm so delighted to be unafraid to use one of those things." So I blew.

Now, I am a smoker (yeah, yeah I know, don't nag . . . I'll kick it eventually) and I have asthma so I couldn't normally even blow up a balloon. My first attempt didn't register on the doodah at all.

"You really are going to have to blow harder. If it doesn't register I'll have to take you to the station."

I had promised I would open a meeting room in town for a support group on Christmas morning and under no circumstances was I going to let those people down. I blew with all my might and of course it was as clear and sweet as a bell! The Garda wished me a Happy Christmas and safe driving and, do you know, it settled my nerves and I drove over to collect the key smiling away to myself.

Having been up since 5 a.m. Christmas Eve morning, I finally closed the hall door of my freezing flat at 4a.m. Christmas Day morning, to be greeted by a frantic Lulu who had left me several little messages around the floor.

Christmas Day I was up, showered, dressed and down at the meeting room in plenty of time. As soon as the meeting was over I switched my phone back on and it rang almost immediately. It was Ava.

"Hi! Just ringing to wish you Happy Christmas!" She sounded all happy and excited.

"Oh thank you, darling. I wish I could see you today," I said.

"Well, you can," she said. "We're just around the corner!"

Wasn't that just the best present any parent ever got on Christmas morning?

So that's the last chapter of my story. For now anyway. And now everybody will know me and nobody will know me. Like us all – but I think at least I know myself at this stage, and that's all that matters.

It has been a long, always interesting but sometimes very unhappy journey I have taken to get to this point in my life. I hope the next few decades are happier than the first five have been. I think they will be.

And remember. One day at a time.

We all Breathe
for Rebecca from your sister

Washed up on Soho shores
The city streets were kind to me
The red lights and street fights
Addictions their dealers in debris

Chorus
Don't look at me like I'm a freak show
What I have been through you'll never know
Why's it so hard for you to see
I'm just like you and you're just like me
We all breathe . . .

The scars are all hidden
They're under my skin behind a wall
So I'll wear a mask (I'll wear a mask)
Just keep on walking, leave the past behind me,
so no one can find me

Chorus

M8

Just because I don't look like you (We all love)

I have the right to be here too (We all cry)

Don't judge me till you've walked in my shoes
(We all bleed)

Do you wanna see the truth? (We all lie, we all
feel, we all try)

Our Lady she guides me now

She says that my sorrows make me strong

That I am forgiven

And one day her son will take me home

Chorus repeat fade out

LYRICS BY HANNAH GRACE DELLER

APPENDIX

The Science Bits

Reference books, research papers and some useful websites on the subject of intersexuality are listed below.

WILLIAM REINER M.D.
'To be Male or Female – That is the Question'
151 Arch Pediatr Adolescent Med. 225 (1997)

JOHN COLAPINTO
'As Nature Made Him: The Boy Who Was Raised as a Girl' – Harper Collins

PROFESSOR MILTON DIAMOND PH.D.
'Sex and Gender are Different: Sexual Identity and Gender Identity are Different'

JANE SPALDING
'What Do Children Know?'

Websites:

www.wikepedia.com   Intersexuality

www.femmefever.com

www.lynneconway.com

"Labels give the illusion of standing for something real, but when we probe deeper, they sort of evaporate. We are what we do, what we feel, how we behave and what trajectory we follow. We are a 'work in progress', as all human beings are. We cannot be defined once and for all by having a label pinned on us.

Both straight and GLBT communities are increasingly recognising that human variations and combinations of this type are not so uncommon, and are honouring them without any need to assign narrow sexuality or gender labels."

From Lynne Conway's website, see above

POOLBEG WISHES TO

THANK YOU

for buying a Poolbeg book.
As a loyal customer we will give you
10% OFF (and free postage*)
on any book bought on our website
www.poolbeg.com

Select the book(s) you wish to buy
and click to checkout.

Then click on the 'Add a Coupon' button
(located under 'Checkout') and enter
this coupon code

USMWR15173

(Not valid with any other offer!)

WHY NOT JOIN OUR MAILING LIST
@ www.poolbeg.com and get some
fantastic offers on Poolbeg books

*See website for details